THE TEACHING PRESS
AT UW-GREEN BAY

About This Book

This book was designed and edited by interns at The Teaching Press at UW-Green Bay. The Project Manager was Sabrina Sodermark. The Book Designer was Kori Koehler, while Shianne Draganowski was the Chief Copyeditor. The The Press Manager for Summer and Fall 2021 was Danielle Lemke. The Director of the Teaching Press is Dr. Rebecca Meacham.

About the Teaching Press at UW-Green Bay

The Teaching Press is a student-managed printing house at the University of Wisconsin-Green Bay. We provide hands-on opportunities for undergraduates to learn transferable skills in a variety of interdisciplinary fields, including writing, budgeting, editing, marketing, project management, workflow, and graphic design. Our mission is to showcase voices in the Northeast Wisconsin region and welcome authors of all fields and origins. Above all else, we value the partnership between our clients and the students working with the press.

For the latest information on our titles and authors, visit
https://teachpress.courses.uwgb.org.

The Golden Age

of Brown County Enterprise

Table Of Contents

Foreword   1

Why This Book   3

Ron Weyers and Wally Hillard:
American Medical Security   16

Paul Shierl: Fort Howard Paper Corp.   40

Dick Resch: KI   62

Don Schneider: Schneider National   92

Bob Bush: Schreiber Foods   118

Takeaways   147

Appendices   154

Acknowledgements   161

Foreword

I have had the good fortune, like many of you, to be both an involved yet detached observer of the business economy during the last forty to fifty years—by any measure the most dynamic and changing of any era. We've lived through it and are living with it.

We've watched unimaginable scientific breakthroughs that have brought us CRISPR and Immunotherapy, combining to deal with the Covid-19 Pandemic. And deep, new, more moral, efficient, and effective, ways of leading and managing our organizations and treating people. There's technology. The refining of how those "bits" can be combined and made even more miniscule to accomplish incredible analyses. It has been a magnificent period in which to live and continually adapt.

It's so good, that there is time to dwell on its negatives, the "unanticipated consequences."

I've had the good fortune, courtesy of Tom Lisle and Harry Dennis, to chair several groups of CEOs for thirty years as part of what has become the largest organization of this kind in the world, founded in Milwaukee, called The Executive Committee (TEC) and now Vistage. I've gotten to be involved first-hand in the changes that have occurred over that time.

I've also had the good fortune to do this in Northeast Wisconsin. I've watched first-hand how the simplicity of the life that we have, and the work ethic that was imbued in us, has nurtured an incredible common-sense creativity and a Nike-like "Just Do It" culture.

For years, I felt that our groups here were about two years ahead of most of the country in embracing new practices, and in avoiding the business culture clutter that most of the rest of the country had to cut through. We just did it.

I no longer feel that way, nor do many others. It's probably because so many other areas have embraced technologic innovations quicker and more effectively than we have. It's a change we're not leading. Perhaps because we don't have to—yet. We are succeeding solidly by pursuing the gilded path that we're on.

There was a time, not long ago, when we had companies here that were truly miraculous in what they did. Both by growing monumentally (by thousands of employees) and by changing their industries with their innovations.

This book exists because some of those stories, representative ones, need to be chronicled so that that heyday doesn't get lost. I am focusing on five of them—there are more. There are small ones, which were very innovative and thrived, but didn't grow by thousands. There are family-owned ones that have persisted through the generations by embracing change. There are entrepreneurs who spawned other entrepreneurs. There are CEOs, who although imperfect people, galvanized their leadership team members who energized their workforces to create these amazing enterprises. It's useful to understand all of these people as people.

There are things to be learned from them. To reinforce. To stimulate thinking that may result in improvement.

Enjoy reading these stories. Appreciate the people who made these stories happen.

Phil Hauck
Fall 2021

Why This Book

Fast Growth is often chaotic, and as a leader lost in the chaos, you often don't have time to develop perspective on what you're doing. At the same time, competition is usually keen, and you're running as fast as you can, and that's the best you can do. Finally, later, you look back and take stock and while you're weary, and there are still faults to find, you can see that you and your team have done something remarkable. You've innovated and dominated in ways you never foretold. And it's really cool!

I've always thought that Northeast Wisconsin, for its small size, has had a slew of companies that have done very creative things on a national scale, and showed the big guys a thing or two—and others who were rock solid through decades and generations. Looking back, the Eighties and Nineties were an extraordinary time for us; even now, years later, the evolution of those organizations continues to be very strong.

It has been kind of a Golden Age.

I'm going to highlight five of those organizations, ones that increased by well more than a thousand employees and created some aspect of dominance on a national level. We'll look at these organizations through meeting and understanding their leaders: how they grew up, what influenced them, what led them to the position of company leader, what drove them, what strategies they followed to dominate, and what aspects of business culture energized the workforce to make it all happen. We'll explore these organizations and these CEOs through the lenses of their key executives who lived these experiences with them.

Hopefully, like me, you will appreciate the insights that these stories offer and recognize the potential within the little commonalities in each chapter:

3

Employers Health/American Medical Security
Ron and Wally at one point had created TWO of the TOP FIVE small business health insurers in the nation.

KI
The furniture maker was the primary supplier to Microsoft and Sun MicroSystems, and today is to Google and Facebook.

Schneider National
One of the largest truckload carriers in the nation, and the forerunner in using satellite technology to track the vehicles. One of very few and the largest that survived the transition from being unionized to non-union when De-Regulation took place.

Schreiber Foods
The primary provider of cheese to McDonald's and many other noted worldwide fast-food companies, and now the second largest yogurt producer in the world.

Fort Howard
Now known as Georgia Pacific, was THE low-cost provider of paper goods (including toilet paper, of course) in the world and likely still is. Today, they have earned the right to be the worldwide transportation coordination headquarters of the entire Koch Industries paper empire.

But they aren't the only ones ... just among the biggest. In any look at that time, you have to include:

Associated Bank Corp
As Kellogg Bank became dominant under Jake Rose, who also spearheaded the drive that brought UWGB to Green Bay. Nick Conlon took over the bank when it had $700 million in assets, and when he retired, it had $14 billion and operated in three states. Today, after Bob Gallagher's cost control leadership and Phil Flynn's strategic, turnaround mind, it has $25 billion in assets.

Marinette Marine
Dwindled to only 40 employees before Dan Gulling took charge and got a Coast Guard cutter contract, then another, then another ... grew to 600 employees and had it on track from surviving to thriving. Sold to Manitowoc Company's Marine division, and then to the Italian shipbuilder, Fincantieri Marine. Employment now fluctuates between 1,000-1,500, and is again the mainstay of the Marinette community.

Ariens
Truly a family business begun in 1933 by Henry Ariens and continued to produce durable lawn mowers and snow-blowers for myriad markets under the auspices of Mike Ariens, and now his son, Dan. Adapted as needed by market requirements and opportunities into new uses, new geographies, and new distribution channels. Now with more than 1500 employees in the U.S., UK, and Norway.

PCMC
Formed in 1919 as Bay City Machine Co., it re-constituted as Paper Converting Machine Corp. in 1923. It's growth and dominance in developing paper-making machinery worldwide began in 1946 under L.G. Wood, expanded further by the Baer family. In 2005, they sold the company to machinery conglomerate Barry-Wehmiller. Today, it has more than 1000 employees, including the Hudson Sharp and Northern Engraving units in Green Bay.

Foth & Van Dyke
Now Foth Group, blossomed and solidified under the strategic mind of Steve Van Dyke, then was taken to much higher levels via 15+ acquisitions and a comprehensive leadership development program by Tim Weyenberg. Today, it employs more than 600 engineers in more than 20 offices across the U.S., under current CEO Randy Homel.

The Meat Packers
• Packerland Packing
Founded in 1960, owned for a while by Colorado ski resort magnate George Gillette of Racine, and at its peak had more than 3,500 employees in four plants. It was purchased by JBS, the world's largest, Brazil-headquartered meat packer.

• American Foods Group
Born Green Bay Dressed Beef, traces its recent history to 1985, when Green Bay attorney Carl Kuehne purchased and grew it, renaming it as American Foods Group. In 2005, for risk protection reasons, he joined with the larger Minnesota Rosen's family meat operations, which then transferred its headquarters to Green Bay. Today, it's a $2 billion business with operations in eight states, and exports to 40 countries.

Enzymatic Therapy
Now Nature's Way, Terry Lemorand created Enzymatic from scratch because healthy nutrition saved him from obesity, and grew it to a healthy organization with products in stores across the nation. After Terry retired, Randy Rose and his successor, Mike Devereux, under some private equity owners but now with a strategic German owner, as Nature's Way have expanded into the Walmarts and Amazons, reaching more than $400 million in sales. Later, Terry created another company, Europharma USA, right next to it in the I-43 Industrial Park.

Integrys Energy Services
Mark Radtke took WPS/Integrys' de-regulated division from infancy to more than $10 billion in flow-through volume, ranking 3rd in the U.S., and a very high scoring, energized culture. Dan Verbanec developed its industry-leading software system, and when it was sold to Constellation, the largest in the country, the IT headquarters was transferred to Green Bay.

Milk Source
Now one of the ten largest dairy operations in the nation with operations in Wisconsin, Illinois, Michigan and Nebraska. Founded in 1999 by three UW-Madison graduates, each of whom grew up on a family dairy farm and understood that the future of dairy agriculture resided in scale. Today, Jim Ostrom is CEO, John Vosters manages the livestock, and Todd Willer handles facility and farming operations. In 2014, Milksource was named the nation's Innovative Dairy Farm of the Year.

Green Bay Packaging
Quietly since 1933, the Kresses, George, Jim and now Will, have created a solid, nationwide supplier of cardboard-related products, one of the first in its industry to cultivate environmental practices and products, culminating in investing in a continuing future with a $500 million paper machine expansion, the first in two decades in the industry.

WS Packaging Group
Located in Algoma as a label printer, Terry Fulwiler took it over from his father when it was at $4 million, and grew it to $400 million through strategic acquisitions, with plants all over the nation, before it was sold. Now headquartered in Green Bay.

Shade Information Systems
Bob Shade was an opportunist/entrepreneur, who jumped into the computer printer paper explosion in the 1970's, becoming a preferred provider in truckload quantities. He is renowned for the company he created, but even more so for nurturing and spawning executives who went on to lead in CEO and other senior positions at almost 30 other N.E.W. companies, including:

Bruce Bell, who founded Belmark, the vast label-printing company now with more than a thousand employees, run by his son-in-law, Karl Schmidt.

Craig Dickman, who founded Breakthrough Technologies, which decreases fuel costs for major shippers, and now heads Titletown Tech, the Microsoft/Packers-sponsored technology innovator.

Jack Riopelle, who became CEO of a franchise-based computer business, then CEO of two paper manufacturers, before joining Wisconsin Film & Bag and making it a force in the plastic bag industry.

Jim Feeney, who became CEO of Wisconsin Film & Bag, succeeding Jack Riopelle.

Bob Rupp, who became CEO of American Finishing Resources, Appleton International, MCL Industries, and others.

Lenny Shefchik, who co-founded Paper Transport, now a 1000-driver trucking company.

Tom Tess, who became part-owner and operator of a school bus franchise.

Glen Yurjevich, who became CEO of Creating Forming, Whitefield Industrial Coatings, Outlook Group and GLC Minerals.

And others, who went on to key executive positions in growing companies.

Says one graduate of Bob Shade's development organization: "He was brilliant; he had a great capacity to see and think strategically. As a micro-manager, he was also difficult to work for sometimes. But he kept great people around him because he gave them responsibility and authority, the freedom to learn, to make mistakes and make progress. The challenges and conversations with him were great. He always had breakthrough ideas: One was a Photovoltaics lab because the ability of the sun to create electricity looked like it would impact some future product possibilities. It didn't work and it was expensive. Others, though, became our new product offerings.

"A fun thing: He was friends with Ross Perot and Jack Welch. The three of them knew each other when they worked at IBM together in their twenties. We could go up to Bob's office in

DePere, and Jack Welch would be in his office with his retinue waiting outside. Bob became IBM's youngest branch manager." And speaking of IBM, IBM had a significant sales office in Green Bay and wanted to use its general managership as a training ground for hot prospects. The problem: The hot prospects liked Green Bay, and often wouldn't move to the next post, leaving IBM. Same with P&G site leaders. Several stayed in Green Bay rather than going to Cincinnati for their next position or Vice-Presidency.

And don't forget the hospitals.

Green Bay is an unlikely place to have three health systems and four hospitals and the attendant clinics and other medical care facilities. We have it because we also serve the huge swath of people north of us, and because of three diverse entrepreneurial initiatives that created them. Together, they account for more than 5,000 employees today:

Bellin

Dr. Julius Bellin founded the Deaconess Sanitarium in 1908 and moved it into a hospital in 1915; it was renamed Bellin Memorial Hospital in 1925. It is locally owned, not owned by or with another organization. In 2005, it was a pioneer in robotic-assisted surgeries.

St Vincent's and St. Mary's

St. Vincent's was formed in 1888 by the Sisters of the Third Order of St. Francis, located in Springfield, Illinois ... and is still operated by them today as a nonprofit, Catholic system. Its first entry into "high-tech" was installation of an elevator in 1903. St. Mary's was created in 1900 by the Misericorde Sisters of Montreal, Canada, to serve unwed mothers and their babies. The St. Franciscan Sisters took over ownership in 1973. Prevea Health is a coalition of doctors created about 1995 as a response to health system consolidation trends. Prevea included doctors in the Webster and West Side Clinics and aligned with the St. Vincent's and St. Mary's hospitals. Today, the hospitals are operated as a division of the Hospital Sisters Hospital System and include other Wisconsin hospital groups.

Aurora

Actually, Aurora was attracted here to align with the BayCare Clinic, created by a group of specialists who didn't want to align with non-profit Bellin and the Sisters, and wanted their own for-profit entity. The Aurora facility in Green Bay is the only one of Aurora's health systems' empire that is for-profit. It's offerings and services are highly rated.

Not everyone was so fortunate, however.

Green Bay's retail dominance didn't survive the chaos created by the big box stores, and then Amazon.

Shopko

Begun with one store in 1962, Jim Ruben expanded like a Target and Walmart, thriving in smaller town locations throughout the country. It expanded organically and through acquisitions to almost 250 stores nationwide with 18,000 employees ... and innovatively by adding pharmacies and optical departments, and other divisions that provided health benefits to organizations. It succumbed, via private equity owners, to overwhelming debt and declining margins due to the competitive online vs. bricks-and-mortar trend.

Prange's

The dominant department store in N.E.W. for decades, with premier stores in Green Bay, Appleton and Sheboygan, followed industry expansion by establishing smaller Prange's department stores in malls in a dozen other nearby cities, and followed the discount store trend with Prange-Way. They eventually succumbed, Prange's to low volume yielding losses in the mall locations, and Prange-Way to the Targets, Walmarts and other successful discounters. Its specialty store operation survived for a while, but only awhile.

There were others, too. Maybe smaller, but led by not untypical Northeast Wisconsin entrepreneurial and persistent minds:

Romo Printing
Fred Darling brought this label printer up from Racine and began building it with major clients like Schneider, Ariens and Mercury Marine/Brunswick. Always looking for a growing niche, he explored nanotechnology early on and found it's attributes could support harder, more long-lasting labels. Now, they are Romo Durable Graphics, and led their industry in embedding RFID chips into labels and embedding labels into plastic parts. Son Jon has led the company's recent growth.

WG&R Furniture
Remember "A mile from downtown, 'tis true, but a mile from high prices, too." Founded in 1946, and taken over by the Greene family in 1955, it's been a staple over time. Entrepreneurial, opened a mattress manufacturing facility in 1984 serving a wide variety of other brand names; created its high-end August Haven brand. Today, led by grandson Jim Greene.

LaForce Hardware
Founded in 1954 by Joe LaForce, and quietly grew through the decades, expanding into other northern Midwest states and Texas.

Amerhart Building Supply Distributor
Tracing its roots to 1940, much of its expansion under the Kasper family ownership occurred since the 1980s, with acquisitions of comparable distributors in five other states.

Bay Industries
Arnie Schroeder created this garage door retailer and construction pipe and other materials distributor and expanded it nationally to more than 90 locations across the country. It's now run by his son, Dan.

Pomp's Tire
Founded in 1939 by "Sparky" Pomprowitz and expanded by new owner Roger Wochinske to a second location in 1965, the organization now has 120 locations in 11 states, plus 18 retread plants and several manufacturing facilities. Still managed by the Wochinski family.

The Green Bay Packers
Of course, the Green Bay Packers, for which the Green Bay area is notorious worldwide, has grown, too, needfully so to ensure that the smallest professional sports market in the world might survive and thrive. At one point, during this period its office staff was 80; today it is about 400, half of them part-time. That's the non-football staff. You don't survive as one of the premier global brands without a formidable social media presence—also reflected in its Pro Shop sales growth!

How They Use Their Wealth

These organizations, and their leaders and other employees, make money. That money forms the economy of the Green Bay area, and most visible is the impact that leaders have had with their developed wealth, returning much of it back into the community.

Some of it is through foundations, but most is through family philanthropic trusts, often placed and invested through the Greater Green Bay Community Foundation. It's not hard to see their impacts. The Carol and Robert Bush Art Center at St. Norbert's, Carol's Court at UWGB, the Kress Center at St. Norbert, The Weyers/Hilliard Library in Howard, the Schneider School of Business and Donald J. Schneider Stadium at St. Norbert College, the Resch Center and Resch Family Trail. The list is a lot longer.

But these very visible contributions are the tip of the iceberg. Dick Resch is known to have said many times within the KI management group that, "I made this money here, and I want to leave a large portion of it here." Too, says his long-time executive assistant, Amy Perrault, "Many evenings he would be signing a number of checks to help out people and organizations."

The Cornerstone Foundation

Long-time executives say that the Fort Howard Foundation was "Paul Schierl's Baby", which he used to provide grants to fund key community needs. The Foundation was created in 1953 by Austin Cofrin, with an initial contribution from the company of $25,000, followed by annual contributions, totaling close to $1 million (while Paul continued as CEO).

According to Sheri Prosser, the executive director since 1991, the key funding that makes it what it is today actually came from purchasing 840 shares of Fort Howard stock. With the stock split of 400-1, the value after the offering was about $11 million, an asset base which has grown to today's approximately $30 million even after decades of grants. Since the inception through 2020, over $46 million has been distributed.

Paul was put on the Foundation Board in 1971 and began heading it in 1974. He made sure it was separate from the company, so it wasn't included in any of the ownership changes. Prosser notes that it is a Wisconsin corporation with its own 8-person Board of Trustees who also serve as the grant determiners, and that the Foundation dispenses approximately 5% of the assets each year in grants, as required by the IRS.

Along with many other contributions, a very visible community benefit is Cornerstone's funding of the purchase and development of the Barkhausen Waterfowl Preserve on the shores of Green Bay.

After Paul's retirement from Fort Howard, he initiated a contest performed by local marketing company, Media Management, to select a new name. There were 1400 submissions, three of which suggested Cornerstone Foundation; those suggesters each received $5,000 for their charity of choice.

Paul was also instrumental in working with a group of interested Green Bay donors in creating the Greater Green Bay Community Foundation about 1993, serving as its first president, and also making personal grants through funds he established there.

What To Look For As You Read

Leaders of growing organizations can be neither calm nor politically correct. They are drivers. They are mercurial. They want their organizations to dominate. They will drag that organization "kicking and screaming" if need be. Read between the lines and keep this in mind.

All people are complex, and no less so these leaders. On the one hand, they are all wonderful people. They care about their families, they care about their employees, and they care about what they are creating. They also have a side where they are not accepting and benevolent, and that will get displayed at important and memorable times; they don't like sub-par performance nor repeated mistakes. Unfortunately, those times are often the ones that are remembered and discussed; in turn, they shape a major part of the leader and their organization's reputation.

But I am here to tell you that that is not the essence of these people. The grace of this book is that you will get insights into who they really are on a day-to-day basis from the people who most interacted with them. Read and absorb that. You will be impressed. And perhaps, like me, you will also come to think that we are fortunate people like these took ahold of these organizations and led and pushed them to succeed, creating employment and healthy family lives for thousands of people in our Green Bay community. You will get insights into what formed them as young people, that molded them into the leader each would become.

And yes, I'm prejudiced.

Ron Weyers and Wally Hilliard

We are grateful to the following former executives and others for their insights which created this chapter:

Julie Bartels
Tim Day
Andy Hilliard
Kris Labutzke
John Lochner
Sandy Mathy
Mike Vande Kamp
Bob Weyers
Colleen Weyers
and
Jeff Weyers

Green Bay's Golden Age:
Ron Weyers and Wally Hilliard
American Medical Security

AMS Values:
Grow
Make Money
Have Fun

The Short Version

In the early 1970s, Ron Weyers had discovered that there was an unmet need for health insurance for small companies; the large company market was dominated by Blue Cross Blue Shield out of Milwaukee, and Wisconsin Physicians Service (WPS) out of Madison. The problem was that the plan offerings were fairly standard, with little flexibility for the needs of the smallest organizations, and no incentive to change. Then, Ron was introduced to a frustrated but very educated and driven, self-described "pots, pans and cutlery" salesperson, Wally Hilliard, who was looking for another gig, and they formed an agency. Wally was the salesperson, gone all day everyplace within 100 miles of Green Bay, returning in the evening with proposal and contract needs, and imploring the small staff to stay late and type up and make copies for the next day. Ron oversaw the administration staff as well as doing selling himself. His wife, Colleen, was instrumental in the "Mom and Two Pops" enterprise.

Soon, Ron and Wally were frustrated with the inflexibility of the offerings and discovered that they could purchase a tiny insurer in southern Wisconsin and use its licenses to set up their own insurance company to sell their own insurance product ideas; to provide the reserve capital, they found an insurer and re-insurer. So, as Wisconsin Employers Group, they began selling their own insurance plan products, much better fitting individual company needs than others on the market.

The Weyers home in Freedom, where it all started.

Gradually, as business grew, so did the workforce, spreading out within the Weyers' farmhouse home near Freedom, Wisconsin—into another upstairs room, and into the basement, a total of 17 people in all.

In 1973, they made the decision to leave the farmhouse and purchased property and built a building at the corner of Ridge Rd. and Parkview in Ashwaubenon. Business continued to grow, and in 1976 they built another building next door. Five years after, requiring even more space, they built a white, 188,000-square-foot building further north on Ridge. (It was subsequently occupied by Schneider National, and then Foth & Van Dyke.) Growth really began to accelerate, and in 1984—then at 600 employees—they built the first 180,000-square-foot wing of the huge white complex on Scheuring Rd. in DePere, overlooking Highway 41. By now, it was known as Employers Health Insurance. The building was soon expanded to its current 380,000-square-feet as growth continued. (When they left Employers in 1988, the company had 1,450 employees. Subsequent owners grew it to almost 3,000 employees.)

They had built an operating culture that generated very loyal employees, and set the pattern for how Ron and Wally, two very disparate personalities, worked together and energized an organization.

By 1982, their very fast premium growth had outstripped the capacity to meet the capital reserve requirement, and they sold to American Express' Fireman's Fund, for more money than they thought they would ever

The Employers Health Insurance building in DePere. The first wing was built in 1984, and the others added as the company grew.

have. Health insurance turned out not to be Fireman's Fund's best strategy, so they sold Employers to Lincoln National of Fort Wayne, Indiana. Cultures became grating, and Lincoln National fired Ron and Wally in 1988—*strangely*, without a non-compete agreement.

The AMS building in Howard, constructed in the early 1990s.

It didn't take Wally long to decide to get back into the business (and a bit longer to convince Ron to re-join him).

Working out of a small office building in downtown DePere, they recruited some of their old employees. Not the VP types, but others below that level who knew the business well, and well exemplified the culture they wanted to replicate. Their backer now was their former competitor, Blue Cross Blue Shield United of Wisconsin, as a 50% owner.

They continued to expand, moving into 14 states with regional offices and into the large Regency office building in downtown Green Bay. And as those hallways became full, they built another white-painted 5-story edifice out in Howard. When they sold again in 1996, they had 3,000 employees in that building.

They had been continually re-structuring to support that growth, inventing on the fly how to hire, train and put in service 50-plus new employees a week who could replicate the customer-focusing demeanors they wanted, and trusting in the competence of people thrust into new supervisory positions with only on-the-job training. What allowed that to happen was a set of behaviors and habits that constituted a very energizing culture. As one former leader says, "It was a culture that companies would kill for today."

By 1996, expansion was catching up with them, stressing both financial capacity and financial performance. Blue Cross exercised its option to buy out Ron and Wally, and the investment group it had put together back in 1988. The pair had fully 4/5ths of the 50% ownership share, but all owners as well as many senior managers walked away with very substantial checks.

Going Forward: The culture that sustained AMS under Ron and Wally turned out to be impossible to maintain under subsequent management; performance declined, and Blue Cross eventually sold it to United Health, which took over the building and made it a core call center for many years. Today, as this is written in 2021, United Health is moving to a much smaller building in DePere, and the huge 5-story edifice in Howard will remain empty for a while.

The legacy: At one point, Ron and Wally had created two of the five largest small business health insurers in the United States. (Innovation? I think yes!)

Every time you go to the doctor, you pay a Co-Pay, right? You use an Insurance Card, right?

So does everyone else in America.

They originated with Employers/AMS.

Flexible plans, including self-funded ones, for small employers? Check.

Disrupting the methodology by which doctors were reimbursed? That, too.

Early stages of Wellness programs!

Relationships with Agents? Ron and Wally had both been agents, and knew what they wanted, and how they wanted to be treated. So, they did that. That's why they always had a line of agents interested in working for them.

That philosophy also carried over into the elements that built the energizing, loyalty- building culture: They treated people how they wanted to be treated.

As this is written, Wally, well into his 80s, is in ill health, and Ron recently passed away after a number of years of increasing dementia.

The Early Years

Ron Weyers

Ron was born in Green Bay in 1939 but grew up on a dairy farm outside nearby Seymour, Wisconsin. His Dad, one of 9 siblings, ran the farm, but wasn't exactly partial to it, and after the kids left home, he sold it and began working for construction companies. His mother, a VanVreede, died early, at age 49.

What Ron wasn't partial to was school; he exited Seymour High School at age 17, and for a year worked for a local cheese processing plant, often driving the milk pickup trucks.

At age 18, he joined the military, and was assigned to Fort Bragg as a paratrooper; he eventually made more than 60 jumps.

Colleen, born in 1940 in Freedom (also on a dairy farm) was very social (and still is). Upon graduating high school, she began working for an Appleton bank. She and Ron weren't friends but encountered each other periodically at events. After Ron's three-year hitch finished, they began dating. Ron, though, re-upped in the Army so he could be assigned to Germany, and they conducted a long-distance relationship-building. Finally, in 1962, when Ron returned after two years, before he went back to Fort Bragg to finish his enlistment, they married. Six months later, he was done.

Afterwards, Ron began looking for a job, and friends who were doing well selling whole life insurance suggested that. It wasn't for Ron, but selling term insurance, much more affordable for younger people, was. He became successful at it. Eventually, he and his partner, Ike Warren, began hearing complaints about health insurance from small business owners. They looked into it and began selling that as well.

During this period, Ron and Colleen purchased a small home on a corner of farmland owned by a relative, a few miles outside Freedom. Here, their sons Jeff and Bob were born consecutively in 1963 and 1964.

Sometime in the late 1960s, Ron's brother, Jim, was a water-skiing buddy with a fellow from Green Bay named Wally Hilliard, once a very successful chemicals salesperson who for some reason was now selling, (as he put it) "pots, pans and cutlery," with a side business selling cash registers. Jim introduced Wally to Ron. Wally liked the idea of selling life and health insurance better, and they competed for a few years. When Wally's partner left for the south to get away from bad winters, Wally suggested he and Ron get together, with Wally as the main salesperson, and Ron and Colleen providing the administration. They began operating their own agency, called Business Associates of Northeast Wisconsin, out of the Weyers home near Freedom.

Wally Hilliard

Wally was born in 1932 on a farm outside Durand, Wisconsin, the youngest of three brothers. Very early in Wally's life, his father contracted tuberculosis and died. His mother now had the task of raising the three while running the farm. Wally wasn't completely helpful. In 1937, at the age of five, he was playing with matches in the loft of the barn; it caught fire, and burned to the ground.

Shortly thereafter, his mother sold the farm and they moved into town, where she got a job delivering milk. She eventually re-married and the family relocated to Kenosha, where the stepfather could get a job in the American Motors plant. As a teen, Wally was periodically employed there in low-level jobs.

In his high school years, he became a wrestler, an interest he has retained throughout his life.

After high school, he joined the military for several years; he didn't want to be assigned overseas, so he finagled a way to get out without doing so. At one point, he was going to be assigned to a very small base in northern Canada, which had no opportunities for fun; he finagled his way out of that one, too.

Maturing, he decided to go to college, and enrolled at UW-Madison to become a veterinarian. At the same time, he took a part-time job as a knife salesman, selling cutlery to housewives. While doing this, at an evening Tupperware-like party where he was promoting pots and pans along with the cutlery, he met his wife-to-be, Belvina, who was going to college in Milwaukee. They married in 1956 while he was still in college.

Eventually, he changed majors from veterinary medicine to chemistry, and upon graduation in 1959, he joined Monsanto Corp. as a chemical salesperson, assigned to the New Jersey area near Philadelphia. Their first child, Dan, was born that year.

He was very successful, and Monsanto soon promoted him to the corporate office in St. Louis. Soon after, though, Bel, now with two more children, Julie and Janice, wanted to return to be near her family near Green Bay. They moved to Shawano in 1962. Their son Andy was born in 1963.

Afterwards, he went back to selling cutlery, pots and pans, and eventually, life insurance.

One evening, he pulled into a gas station in Shawano, just as it was closing, and got the attendant, Jim Weyers, to re-open "if you buy a full tank of gas." That meeting evolved into a friendship, and Wally convinced Jim to become an insurance agent as well. Eventually, Jim introduced Wally to his older brother, Ron, who was also an insurance agent, doing well selling health insurance to very small businesses.

After spending time with Ron, Wally thought selling health insurance looked like a better business to be in, and, when Wally's partner left the area for warmer climes, he suggested that Ron (and Colleen) combine forces with him, with Wally focused completely on selling, Ron dividing time between administration and selling, and Colleen keeping the books.

The Road To Employers Health Insurance Company

The Weyers farmland home was quickly adapted into an agency.

"We started with four desks in one room," recalls Colleen, "and I created space for me in another room. We hired a few people to help, people we know. Wally would spend all day selling, returning at end-of-day with requests to write letters and develop proposals, and prepare for the next day. He often wouldn't leave until 10 PM at night. I would call my sisters and ask them to come over at the end of their own workday and help us get stuff out so Ron and Wally could deliver them the next day."

Not long after, Wally and Ron began encountering unique needs of prospects that weren't easily fulfilled with the Blue Cross and WPS products. They wanted more flexibility in what plans they could offer. In short, they needed their own health insurance company.

One complication was that Wisconsin law prevented them from selling to the very smallest, with 2-10 employees, except through a Multi-Employer Trust, effectively a purchasing alliance banding together the smallest companies into a more-easily-administered group. So, they created one—and now needed to be a Third-Party Administrator, which would be called Wisconsin Employers Group.

Ron and Wally took the Management Group on a series of retreats, including fishing expeditions in Canada.

Serendipitously, as they dreamed about this, in southern Wisconsin there became available a small, floundering insurer available for sale, complete with the licenses needed to operate.

Ron and Wally bought the shell. Then, they searched for an organization willing to take the financial risk, eventually discovering Central National Life out of Jacksonville, Illinois, and a reinsurer called CNA out of Chicago. Now, they were in the small business group health insurance business.

Very quickly, they had to staff up while also increasing the selling capability to support it. They needed people to prepare proposals, prepare the plans, do claims processing, prepare checks, and much more. They were simply agents who were now in the very complex, very highly regulated business of providing insurance and needing the reserves to do it—all on the first floor and basement of that farmhouse.

Eventually, the staff rose to 17 people, bursting the basement at the seams. Employees were asked to work late hours, often weekends—whatever was necessary to serve the clients.

But it was all fun. The culture that would later become famous at Employers and AMS began to form itself. The banter was constant even as people applied themselves to the urgent tasks. Special lunches were brought in. If working late, pizza arrived. The refrigerator was kept stocked with beer. Special occasions like birthdays and anniversaries were celebrated. The camaraderie was great. No one left, and others came. A large part of the success was Colleen's ever-welcoming personality, and Ron's constant interest in people and their lives. And especially, the employees' interest in theirs.

"When we were in second and third grade," recalled their son Bob, "we'd come home after school and all the ladies would stop working to talk to us. 'How was school today? What did you do? Aren't you cute!'

But it was all fun. The culture that would later become famous at Employers and AMS began to form itself. The banter was constant even as people applied themselves to the urgent tasks. Special lunches were brought in.

We were a hit. Worked stopped for a whole fifteen minutes."

In 1973, they purchased property at the corner of Ridge Road and Parkview Lane in Ashwaubenon and built a (white again) building there. In 1976, they added another white one next to it.

And as expansion "continued to continue," in 1982, they built an even larger, (can you guess? White!) 188,000 square foot multi-story building two blocks further north on Ridge. The two smaller buildings were eventually occupied by Schneider Communications, and after they left the larger of the two, Schneider National itself moved in as its headquarters; likewise, when Schneider moved out to their huge complex at Packerland and Waube, Foth & Van Dyke moved in as their headquarters—until they, too, moved to a much larger building south of DePere, very visible from Highway 41.

Of interest, the contractor for all the Ron and Wally buildings was James J. Calmes Construction. Jim Calmes was a small contractor from Freedom, a good friend, and Ron and Wally gave him the contract to build the first building, and then the second, and then the much larger third, and then the huge (white!) fourth and then the gigantic (and white!) fifth. He grew as they grew.

During the late 1970s, Employers was becoming more strategic, making acquisitions that broadened the base of insurance offerings they could provide. Client employers wanted to deal with just one agent for all their insurance needs, so Employers developed capabilities for life, vision, dental and others—and in 1979 even auto and homeowners.

By now, the Ron and Wally culture was ingrained. Their stated values were:

Grow
Make Money
Have Fun

Later, these were added:

Fight Communism
Back The Pack

(With emphasis on that third one...)

The key to fun, several said, is that it's integrated into the work, that it's not a committee add-on.

Many departments had their own refrigerators, stocked with soda and beer, and their own coffee pots going all day long. New employees were told not to miss the 4:30 PM "meeting,"—just an informal break in the workday for a few minutes before getting back to it. Decisions were made there, though.

One employee remembers later experiencing Chocolate Milk Day, the "All You Can Eat Bacon Bar (While It Lasts)," Christmas Wrapping parties, $2 lunches, and the 5th Floor Game Room.

Just as in the Weyers home, birthdays and anniversaries were celebrated, as were anything else a person could imagine on an impromptu basis.

Most of it was an extension of Ron.

"He was as genuine as anyone could be. He would wander through the departments talking to people. He knew what the janitor did last weekend and would ask him about it. He knew whose car had broken down. Many late afternoon Fridays, he would pull a dolly up to the refrigerators and re-fill them with soda and beer," explains one employee.

"He was more introverted than people think," says another, "his preference was small groups, or no group—if and when he could have his preference. But his role demanded the opposite, and he was exquisite at it. When in the limelight, whether with a few or many, he was focused on each person to the degree he could be, both interested and supportive. He was fun to be around, and people gravitated to him."

Wally handing out checks at Christmas time.

Halloween was a big day for dressing up and partying. At Christmas time, Ron and Wally would circulate among the people dressed up as Santa Claus and an elf, respectively.

"I remember we were giving every single employee $100," recalls one attendee, "but when we grossed it up to deduct taxes, it came out at $99.99. Wally went around giving everyone the additional penny."

"Our turnover was virtually nil. Thank goodness," laughs another.

But fun must be a genuine extension of other elements of culture.

"They listened. Wally was always going to agents to learn about what they and prospective groups needed. Ron was interested in what each employee felt could be improved. And they acted on these ideas because they were critical to both survival and profitable growth," explains another. They conveyed an attitude of respect for every employee, that every employee had something to offer to create improvements. This was critical. Even as the company grew, it remained nimble (not without some stress to stay together), creating more new insurance products than any competitor. As a result, they were loved by agents.

They listened especially to agents. They would bring groups of them into the Green Bay headquarters for several days at a time, as well as annually in a large group for the Tailgater, which involved a Packer game. The agents were allowed to roam at will through the headquarters, talking to employees, asking them questions, responding to questions, and finding the ones who took care of them and their clients and thanking them, creating the personal relationship that fosters extra effort. At the Tailgater, when agents arrived on Friday afternoon, they had a red carpet into the building with employees lining it to greet them.

They listened especially to agents. They would bring groups of them into the Green Bay headquarters for several days at a time, as well as annually in a large group for the Tailgater, which involved a Packer game.

They didn't micromanage. Employees at all levels, especially at the top, were allowed to do their jobs as best they could, improvising as they went along, creating the next evolution of improvement. They were trusted to perform on behalf of their customers, whether external or internal. The freedom energized. "We were told how to do the job, and how to handle customers, and given back-up—and then told to just do the job the best way we could. Wally would tell the senior team, 'Do what you have to do," says Kris Labutzke, who ran the underwriting department.

Another element, often mentioned, was that people had career improvement to work for. All the growth created new opportunities to become a supervisor, and then a manager, even though it would be on-the-job-training. Wally wasn't the

Kris Labutzke

people-person that Ron was, but he appreciated very much the extra effort that he could see that people put into their jobs.

In the health insurance business, indeed most insurance businesses, there are two parts:

The *operating company*, which does everything, and the *big pockets*, which has the capital to pay claims and back up potential losses. Employers' growth was straining the capability of its backer, so in 1982, it sold to American Express' Fireman's Fund division, located in San Francisco. (The price was a little less than $10 million. Ron and Wally were now employees with incentive contracts.) Fireman's Fund was not primarily a health insurer, so its health business was transferred to Employers fairly quickly.

(Early on after the purchase, American Express' CEO, Sandy Weil, visited Green Bay to better understand the company; part of his entourage was a fast-track intern named Jamie Dimon, who would later become the billionaire CEO of JP Morgan Chase, the nation's largest bank. Eventually, the reporting relationship changed, and the company reported to a New York-based executive named Lou Gerstner, who would lead IBM's major turnaround as CEO. When Gerstner visited Green Bay, he was impressed by the company's Circle of Success recognition program. Winners were people at all levels of the company judged to have done innovative things. The reward: a weekend at Maxwelton Braes resort in Door County, where they and their families were waited on by Ron, Wally, and the entire executive group.)

That created new challenges: how to not only absorb the increased business administratively, but also how to create relationships with Fireman's huge agent base. Who is this little company in Green Bay, they asked? To address that, they created a video, called The Big Event. Agents were issued "ringside seat tickets," and the video depicted the Big Guy with boxing gloves and the Little Guy with boxing gloves—boxing ring, announcer, robes, attendants, everything. The video said that Employers was up to the challenge.

Then, they invited many of the agents to come to Green Bay for a headquarters meeting.

As they got off the buses from the airport, they were greeted to a red carpet, and as they entered the multi-level lobby, employees were on every level above them in sunglasses, singing the new hit song, "The Future Is So Bright I Gotta Wear Shades."

A few years later, Fireman's Fund decided, even though Employers yielded $40-$50 million in underwriting/investment profits annually, that the Ron 'n Wally show was worth more sold, and sold it in late 1986 for $215 million to Lincoln National Life of Fort Wayne, IN, which was heavy into developing HMO networks at the time.

HMO networks have narrow doctor groups, so as to drive more business to that group for a lesser amount of reimbursement per capita, but larger in total, and theoretically would be more focused on the patient's health. Wally was appointed to Lincoln National's management committee and would provide them his evaluation of their decisions. "They were experts at Buying High and Selling Low." Eventually, Lincoln National grew tired of the relationship.

In Spring 1988, they asked Ron and Wally to fly to Fort Wayne for a meeting. Unknown to them, a Lincoln National contingent was walking into the Employers headquarters to notify executives that Ron and Wally had been terminated. "You guys are entrepreneurs, and we aren't. Go out and be entrepreneurs and let us take this," said the Lincoln National CEO. Ron and Wally were flown back to Green Bay and escorted into, and then out of, the Employers building to get their personal things.

"The place was aghast. People couldn't believe their eyes and went into mourning. There were tears," recalls one executive.

Strangely, Lincoln National had not yet completed a Non-Compete Agreement with them.

Two nights later, Ron and Colleen went to only the second movie they'd seen together in ten years. It's title: "A New Life."

Now unemployed and with a large nest of eggs, they went their separate ways to determine their next eras. After getting over the shock, Wally quickly decided he wanted back in the insurance game. He began looking for another insurance company to purchase—to no avail.

He approached Ron to join up together again, but Ron was reluctant, so Wally went ahead. American Medical

Each organization took 50% ownership of the profits (and losses if they occurred). Of AMS' 50%, Ron and Wally took 40%, and 10% was owned by a number of Green Bay investor friends. It would become an excellent investment.

Security began to take shape. Each organization took 50% ownership of the profits (and losses if they occurred). Of AMS' 50%, Ron and Wally took 40%, and 10% was owned by a number of Green Bay investor friends. It would become an excellent investment.

Besides luring key executives from Employers to a single room in downtown DePere's Heritage Building, he had to find that financial backer. Sandy Mathy, Employee #5, recalls cold calling lots of smaller insurers who balance sheet reviews indicated would have capacity. Lots of turndowns. Finally, though, Milwaukee-based Blue Cross Blue Shield of Wisconsin listened. They had a small casualty insurer subsidiary that could be the backer, so they committed. A risk: They would be on the hook for losses if they occurred, with no voice in the AMS operations. But Wally had a well-known track record for growth; Employers had more than 1500 employees when he left.

Ron had taken the bait and rejoined, initially overseeing the massive effort to develop the custom software to drive the business, with all its flexible plans, including upgrades from the Employers system.

Sandy Mathy

They began to recruit the key management team members mostly from the below-VP level at Employers, and most with just one phone call. Kris Labutzke, who became the VP/Underwriting, notes that the day she resigned, the company said as a policy she needed to leave that day. As she was walking out, "people were literally jamming pieces of paper into my pockets with their telephone numbers on them. They wanted to go to the new company."

Kris became employee #6 at AMS.

Eventually, the Heritage building filled with 300 employees, 150 of them from Employers, "and more were eager to."

"Our first-year objective," Kris recalls, "was 6,000 lives." She was allocated three people for underwriting, whom she recruited from Employers. The advantage of hiring there: Everyone was experienced and knew what to do. (Underwriters are the people who, with guidelines, evaluate the risks within a prospective group and assign a price.) Even Regional Managers and Agents joined AMS from Employeita.

Fortunately, a Milwaukee insurer was going bankrupt, and AMS purchased its book of business, which included 22,000 lives, as well as Tim Day, who came up as CFO. The business was off to a healthy start—maybe too healthy.

During this period, a major initiative was to develop the software system that would drive all parts of the insurance processing process. Even now, it's massive and complex. Ron hired a large cohort of programmers, many of them fresh out of UW-Eau Claire, to write the software, often joining it with off-the-shelf modules. The exercise became like the great stories of the intensive efforts by a small group to develop major systems—many

Tim Day

intense, focused, tiring All-Nighters. Not infrequently, as they were working in the De Pere building, knowing they would be going well into the night or all night, a cooler would appear filled with beer, and some pizza deliveries. But they had to keep up with the fast growth of claims, which became a nip-and-tuck effort, often requiring assigning the VPs responsibility for answering the constantly-ringing phones with complaints.

Within a year, they moved to downtown Green Bay to the 5-story Regency Building. Growth continued, as did the chaos. "Growth was outrunning most of the systems, and we didn't have time to upgrade. Shortly after I moved in, my office and that of a VP were moved to create a training room, and we were moved into broom closets. We didn't care. Nobody did," recalls els, who joined the company at the Regency in 1992.

The next year, they moved to the huge Howard complex, because Green Bay's city leaders couldn't agree on a real estate deal to keep them downtown.

"When I joined in 1988," recalls one executive, "other new executives and I said, 'There's no order, no organization, no leadership! It's chaotic!' That's what I thought at first; there were fewer organization meetings than I thought there should be. I waited a bit to analyze the Ron and Wally relationship and watch the results. What I learned was there wasn't chaos at all. It was the most well-engineered business machine I ever experienced. People said they were good entrepreneurs but bad organizationally, and it would eventually collapse around them. Not so at all." They had to constantly re-engineer the software drivers to incorporate new plans and programs, and growth created mistakes, but the cultural will to keep customer-focused over-rode the problems—sort of. Another executive recalls, "At one point, we wanted our mantra to be 'Easy To Do Business With.' Sounds good, but we couldn't get it to work as well as we wanted. When you're fast-growing you have lots of new people. So, many didn't have the experience to help customers quickly or correctly."

The Business

AMS as a business lasted only eight years, from 1988 to 1996. Ultimately, like Employers, AMS became a victim of its own success. The Blue Cross Blue Shield of Wisconsin subsidiary that provided the capital requirement, got stretched by the premium growth. Blue Cross took it public to attract more capital, but that didn't work. Finally, Blue Cross exercised its option to purchase AMS according to a formula agreed to at inception that yielded a major windfall for the Green Bay-based investor team as well as the cohort of key executives. But in eight years, they grew from nothing to 3,000 employees housed in the huge, towering Howard building. "In 1990, we had ten regional managers; in 1996, we had a hundred, including district managers. In 1990, we had $50 million in premium; in 1996, we had $1.5 billion."

On Growth

"We were hiring 50 people a week for a long time. Each Monday morning, the executive team and Ron and Wally would kick off their training with an orientation meeting. It was unimaginable!' Kris Labutzke explains, 'By 1996, I had 300 employees in my department. It worked well because all my managers and all of their supervisors were experienced.

We were hiring 50 people a week for a long time. Each Monday morning, the executive team and Ron and Wally would kick off their training with an orientation meeting. It was unimaginable!

As we hired, the new people could quickly grab our approach to underwriting by how we modeled it."

Mike Vande Kamp notes, "As we moved towards 2,000 people, unemployment was tight and even with the reputation of the culture, it was tough to find people. We asked employees, 'Who in your family would you like to have working here?'" We liked family members and friends of good employees. That got us to 2,000. After that, we began hiring directly from colleges, the UW System including UWGB, St. Norbert, NWTC. So, for many, we were their first job—and they didn't know how good they had it. To train them, we needed to create AMS University, and every cohort included time with Ron and/or Wally talking about the Culture, the behaviors that were expected of them in doing the job.

On Agents

Mike Vande Kamp was responsible for the vast sales organization, working through Regional and District Managers who oversaw brokerages who employed the agents. A very few of them provided virtually half of AMS' premium revenue. "Our objective was to make the people in the field wealthy. If they prosper, then so will the company.

Mike Vande Kamp

"Ron and Wally had been agents themselves, so we were charged with serving agents' needs, and we developed unique abilities to relate to them. One example is the underwriting that sets the pricing for each group. In most companies, if an agent working with a prospective group has a question about a unique situation, he worked through his broker to contact the insurance company. With us, the agent could call his underwriter and talk with her about the group's specific needs. The underwriter's job was to ask questions to understand the risk, and see if a reasonable premium could be set. We always tried to get to Yes. When an agent visited the home office, he would make a beeline for the underwriter to meet her personally, and to thank her. We encouraged that."

"I didn't have to go to a VP or Ron and Wally," says chner, Appleton, who ran one of the largest brokerages. We would often figure it out at the underwriter level. Because of this flexibility, they were like a breath of fresh air. And I not only could attract 2-10 employee customers to change to Employers, but I was able to sell

John Lochner

AMS to some very large organizations like Shopko and Associated Bank, both of which had locations in many states and thousands of employees."

"Even more importantly," adds Lochner, "the employees would want them and told their employers so. This came from special situations, unusual situations in which AMS reacted very positively and quickly to take care of the insured family."

Vande Kamp continued, noting, "We rewarded the best agents very well, giving them membership in our World Council. If you qualified, you and your spouse could participate in our fully funded trips. Over the years, we took them to Acapulco, Aruba, St. Thomas, a Caribbean cruise and to Switzerland. The days would start very early with meetings, so they could have more of the day to be with their spouses doing the fun things. Our Regional and District managers had the potential to be paid very well as well. It depended on the amount of premiums created. The conversation would go like this: 'How much money do you want to make next year?' We then worked with them to develop a plan to achieve the premium levels necessary to get them there."

On Innovation

Vande Kamp explains, "We were a forerunner in the industry for several things. The insurance card you carry actually came from AMS. Also, the idea of Co-Pays, and another was developing self-funding for small groups. The main one, though, he reiterates, was using the flexibility of software and actuarial judgement to allow customized plans for groups. We were way ahead of our competition. The objective was to create an 'Unfair Advantage,' one that would 'keep us off the prospective group's spread sheets' where the only differentiator was price."

Indeed, Employers/AMS was the **first to apply the idea of Co-Pays in the broader market**, giving the patient "skin in the game" when they make a decision to go to the doctor's office or the hospital (and lowering premiums), which is now ubiquitous in the industry. Too, it was always a quandary to figure out how/whether a small group could self-insure, take on its own risks to lower the cost of insurance. At what point, and for what cost tradeoffs? They developed approaches to do this.

Your Insurance Card

Originally, after each time with a doctor, you received an invoice and a claim form to complete and return to get your reimbursement. Very complicated for the insured. Why not simply have a card with your unique number, provide that to the doctor, and let that drive the reimbursement process with the insuror.

Self-Funding For Small Groups

Not that hard. It's a matter of pricing after analyzing the risk in the context of your entire premium base. It stretched the target market for AMS agents to groups as small as 80 employees.

If you want to attract agents to your plans, and serve their needs with their prospects and clients, make it so that your plans are **adaptable to as many situations as possible.** You over-run the competition that way, and that's what AMS did. Its prices were typically a tad lower than others, too. Even an employer with just four employees could get a plan with four customized choices.

Julie Bartels

Julie Bartels, who had the position of being the ombudsman between marketing/communications and IT to make new products happen recalls, "Often, a new plan would come to us on a piece of napkin, be reviewed by Wally, Sandy Mathy and Mike Vande Kamp, and then we'd start asking all the questions to figure out what it was so we could make it happen and get it into the field."

Most ideas came from listening to agents, and then the brains of Wally and Sandy Mathy, the product development guru. She had responsibility for all four legs of the product development and delivery process. As Wally said, "OATK: One Ass To Kick." She says, "By far the biggest reason for our success was our ability to innovate. And when you innovate, you make mistakes, some bad decisions. I remember Wally walking into my office one day after I had blown something, and saying, 'Sandy, in some cultures, when people do bad things, they get their hands cut off, or their tongues cut off if they say bad things. I want you to think that your fingertips have now been shortened, but I don't want you to stop trying new ideas,' We could make mistakes, and would hear about it, but we would learn and keep going."

> *By far the biggest reason for our success was our ability to innovate. And when you innovate, you make mistakes, some bad decisions.*

More from Mathy:

This was the early stages of using 800 Numbers. We created a call center using 1-800-U-CAN-ASK that policy holders could call, and 1-800-EASYRAT(E) that agents could call.

We knew that with a dinner and a bottle of wine, we could learn a lot about what was happening in the marketplace. At one point, we were in Denver, and the head of the local PPO said they were getting killed by Kaiser Permanente, the HMO king, which was charging Co-Pays when insureds went to the doctor for service, with much lower premiums charged to the employer. We listened and quickly developed our own Co-Pay program—the first in the nation applied to the PPO market, a much larger market. We also looked at benefits that others didn't, such as inclusion of chiropractors/naturopaths in our plans.

We were one of the first to institute use of health/fitness assessments as an incentive technique to lower premiums. If a person took a biometric assessment, and showed other behaviors known to lower service levels, our Lifestyle Choices plan would provide lower costs.

We learned that PPO heads, because they negotiate directly with the doctors and hospital groups, knew pricing trends early. So instead of waiting for claims history to tell us, and be two years behind the curve, we could change our pricing much earlier.

Tim Day notes, "To say Wally Hilliard was an idea person is a massive understatement. He had more ideas by Noon than most people do in a lifetime. It was Sandy and Ron's job to sort through them. Here's how Ron said he dealt with Wally: 'I listen and nod my head, and forget about it. If the same idea is broached a second time, I give the same reaction. But if he comes in a THIRD time with the same idea, then I pay attention. I create a conversation and explore it to see if it's worth looking at further.'"

"Wally loved the interplay of ideas. He was analytical, an intellectual. You needed to be sharp to be around him, and he appreciated people who were thinkers and debaters. He wasn't reluctant to question, to listen, to confront, to debate, to learn."

Two groups who bore his brunt were doctors and medical organization negotiators, whom he faced in negotiating how much to reimburse for their services. One executive explains, "Typically, negotiations with medical systems on pricing would focus on how high above the Medicare rate the insurer would pay for particular services. The medical systems had to accept the federally mandated Medicare pricing, so they were absorbing that, usually at a loss, and desired to make it up by charging private payers more, much more—usually in the range of 200% of Medicare. Wally would have none of that. 'You accept Medicare, so your costs can't be too much above that, and you're living pretty well. Let's talk about 125%.' Sometimes they would end up there, sometimes at 150%. But AMS would often be paying lower reimbursements and capturing larger margins'. Wally had no compunction about going after doctors."

Additional Comments On Ron and Wally

• "You had to understand Wally, and most people didn't. He would often make a crazy statement to you, but that was his way of asking a question as to whether the idea was a good one or not. He wants you to come back with your questions, your counterpoints. You had to be secure in his "

• Wally was brilliant, always out front. He could figure out things well before anyone else could, and as a result often had difficulty getting buy-in. When HillaryCare was being developed in 1993-1994, he attended a meeting of the Health Insurance Assn. of America to discuss how it was developing and what they should be including. He told them they couldn't wait to see how Guaranteed Issue might work and impact them. They needed to be part of the discussion, to lead. They didn't, and they should have." Sandy adds, "As we were waiting outside Senator Dole's office to talk about it with him, Wally said to me, 'Whoever would have thought that a guy from Shawano would have a voice in creating a national health care plan.'" Of course, HillaryCare failed to be implemented.

• Another Wally idea: "An unemployed person typically can't afford COBRA, but if we were to apply a 1% tax on the Unemployment Compensation pool, it would provide sufficient health insurance for the unemployed. He was right. But it went nowhere."

Wally and Ron in an informal moment.

• "People said they worked well together. Not necessarily so. Each had his major set of responsibilities, which in a fast-growing company are all-consuming. What was superb is that when they saw they weren't in sync, they took the initiative (usually at Ron's behest) to sit down and get aligned again. Usually, Wally would move more towards Ron's viewpoint because Wally's ideas had to work in the operating world which Ron coordinated."

• "Wally never 'told' you what to do. But he would keep trying to convince you about how good his idea was and that you should embrace and do it. Sometimes we would say to him, 'Okay, just tell me to do it!' He still wouldn't."

- "Wally couldn't sit still. Even after they sold AMS, he would call and say, 'Let's start another company.'"
- They hired lots of women; 80% of the workforce at AMS were women. "They felt like women were often more effective than men because they were more caring and attentive to detail."

- "They absolutely needed each other. Wally was the idea person; Ron would implement. When Ron recognized one of Wally's good ideas, he would ask many questions about it, look at it from different perspectives, and then create a team to make it happen. He would be part of that team, and would make the project fun."

- "Wally cared about people, but because he focused on new ideas and progress, he didn't show it as well as Ron. He was smart, but also kind and generous."

- "Ron was an unbelievable administrator. He could really pull people together in teams to make things happen. He would make a process out of chaos, even when sometimes you couldn't understand how it was happening."

- "Ron took Management by Walking Around to an art. If someone was being mistreated, or something could be done better, Ron found out about it and fixed it."

Finally, says a long-time broker and friend:

> *"For Ron and Wally, it wasn't about the money.*
> *It was about the game."*

Paul Schierl

*We are grateful to the following for their insights
from their experiences which created this chapter:*
Cliff Bowers
Don DeMeuse
George Hartmann
Kathleen Hempel
Sheri Prosser
Tim Reilly
Mike Riordan
Jim Schoshinski
Susan Schierl Sullivan

*The University of Wisconsin-Green Bay's Archives
Division also hosts comprehensive memorabilia
from the Fort Howard ownership period, which
we accessed for annual reports of financial data,
photos, articles, and other background, including
the LBO Prospectus.*

Green Bay's Golden Age:
Paul Shierl
Fort Howard Paper Corp.

"Concentrate on what we do best, and do it better than anyone else."
~Paul Shierl, CEO (1974-1990)
1982 Annual Report

To understand what Fort Howard Corp. did and still does best, which is to produce paper towels, napkins and bath tissue more efficiently than anyone else in the industry, you have to go back to its founder in 1919, Austin Cofrin.

He was an extraordinarily entrepreneurial, resourceful, imaginative, and committed human being. In 1919, he and some employees left another paper producer in Green Bay to start their own on the west side of the Fox River, and like all beginning enterprises, they did all they could to minimize costs by doing everything they could themselves.

They created a machine shop to service the mill equipment, and eventually used it to build converting machines to supplement ones he bought on auction and refurbished. With his engineering mind, he would watch machines operate, and figure out ways to reconfigure them to operate faster or otherwise more cost-effectively. They mixed their own chemicals, generated their own power, and developed their own landfills for waste.

But most importantly, they used recycled wastepaper to lower the raw material cost decades before it became de rigueur. They purchased their first wastepaper railcar in the mid-1930s, a full 50 years before recycling achieved

But most importantly, they used recycled wastepaper to lower the raw material cost decades before it became de rigueur. They purchased their first wastepaper railcar in the mid-1930s, a full 50 years before recycling achieved mainstream interest.

mainstream interest. Their differentiator was figuring out new, cost-lowering de-inking technologies.

These new practices and solutions differentiated them from competitors, and to protect these advantages, he adopted a corporate stance of secrecy. Fort Howard truly evolved as The Fort, impregnable. "It became known as a great place to work, 'if you can get in.'" Austin Cofrin took good care of his employees, as did his son John, CEO from 1970 until his untimely death in 1974, and so did Paul Schierl, his successor who grew the company dynamically from 1974 to his retirement due to ill health in 1990. Employees appreciated the year-end "Goodwill Bonus." Ten percent, and sometimes up to 19%, of an employee's pay were gifted at year-end, depending on company profit performance—a very anticipated event.

Fort Howard became a public company in 1971 to take care of legacy shareholders who wanted to cash out.

When Paul Schierl became CEO in 1974, revenues were $200 million, double that of only four years earlier, but with net income before taxes of $37 million, a remarkably high percentage for the industry. Its products were paper napkins, towels, and bath tissue for the commercial marketplace (hotels, offices, restaurants).

The marketing challenge was to sell the capacity, and as a public company, the challenge became to increase capacity. Paul Schierl's boldest decisions, executives of that era say, were to expand to two remote locations with huge new paper-making facilities in 1976 in Muskogee, Oklahoma, and in 1986 near Savannah, Georgia. These both had 300-inch-wide machines, the largest and most efficient in the world, and each represented close to $500 million investments. They would service the Western and Southeastern markets, saving tens of millions in trucking costs. They provided the capacity for the Fort Howard tissue business to reach the $1.2 billion in revenue mark by Schierl's retirement in 1990. Employment then in Green Bay was around 4,000, plus 1,000 at each of the two remote plants. Today, as Georgia Pacific and owned by Koch Industries, the plants produce 30% more in production volume with fewer employees.

The 1980s continued Paul Schierl's bold moves. What looked excellent strategically, turned out not to be. A cash-flush organization in a time of very high interest rates, Fort Howard made the very bold move in 1983 to purchase the much larger and well-respected Maryland Cup Corp., maker of the well-known Sweetheart brand of disposable plates and utensils … a good strategy move. That added more than $600 million in sales and more than 10,000 employees. Two years later, they added the famous Lily Tulip Corp., adding another $300 million and 3,000 employees.

It also added an investment of $800 million.

Both companies had outdated plants all over the world and were struggling for profitability. The idea was to invest in modernizing the plants, get them to embrace Fort Howard's culture of cost efficiency, and dramatically improve margins and pricing while leveraging their good brand names.

Fort Howard was now in the consumer goods business. Schierl moved quickly to invest additionally in new plants in England and Hong Kong, and to upgrade machines throughout.

The common denominator in all of Paul Schierl's efforts, supporting the goal of maximum cost efficiency, was paper-making guru Don DeMeuse who oversaw all operations, plant expansions and machine innovations during Schierl's tenure— and who succeeded him as CEO in 1990.

Don DeMeuse

But the Cup foray didn't work. Imposing the frugal Fort Howard culture on businesses that had been run loosely, didn't have good processes or procedures, were consumer-oriented which the Fort had little understanding of, and partially operated with unionized workforces, didn't go well. It became impossible to mesh the various cultures.

Cost cutting eventually reduced Cup division payroll by 6,000 people, to about 8,000. (In Baltimore, where Maryland Cup's headquarters was, the impact of the cuts and attendant policies, as you can imagine, was not well received.)

In 1989, the Cup business would be spun off as Sweetheart Holdings for $620 million, a significant loss on the $868 invested in it; in 2004 it was purchased by Solo Cup, Chicago.

In the late 1980s, Schierl was concerned about the low stock price, which could result in a hostile takeover of the company by an outside organization, and which he didn't want because it would likely destroy the culture, remove a headquarters from Green Bay, and lead to a reduction in headquarters jobs. Despite the Cup challenges, the basic tissue business was still a major money-maker.

He began working with the Morgan Stanley private equity organization to undertake a fairly new technique referred to as Leveraged BuyOut, where the buyer would use substantial debt to purchase the company and then pay off the debt by improved business results over the next years. In 1988, Morgan Stanley Capital and its parent became the 73.5% owner of Fort Howard, taking on $3.6 billion in debt and its massive annual interest payments.

During the negotiations, Schierl suffered a heart attack which sidelined him awhile. Then, in 1990, at age 55, he suffered another heart attack and was being treated at the Cleveland Clinic when he suffered a stroke. Shortly after that, he announced his retirement and the appointment of Don DeMeuse to succeed him as CEO, under the ownership of Morgan Stanley Capital.

The following years were eventful. New products were developed, especially environmentally conscious ones taking advantage of the recycling capability, and machinery upgrades and expansions continued. While operating earnings thrived, the remaining debt and its attendant interest expense would result in negative net income. Morgan Stanley Capital wanted out. In the 90s, they took the company public again, using some of the proceeds to pay down expensive debt and selling some of their stock holdings as the stock price increased. With dynamic financial results (sales increased 32% in 1996 with continuing high margins), they sold Fort Howard in 1997 to James River, the gigantic consumer paper products maker. Mike Riordan, who succeeded Don DeMeuse as CEO, became Fort James' President/COO for a year. Fort James had its own challenges, and was purchased by Georgia-Pacific, also a big player in the tissue business, in 2003. At that time, there were 4,000 employees in Green Bay.

Mike Riordan

While the number of employees has dropped due to efficiencies, GP has maintained the investment commitments to the plants to insure it remains a world-class performer. The purchase of GP by Koch Industries in 2005 hasn't impaired that commitment. Indeed, the entire Koch Industries colossus' logistics are coordinated from Green Bay today, operating as KBX.

The Early Years

Paul Schierl was born in 1935 in Menasha, WI, in the middle of the Depression. In 1939, when he was four, his father was killed in a car accident, and his mother raised her two boys as a single parent, working full-time at the nearby Marathon paper mill as the Depression ended and WWII enveloped all life. His daughter, Susan Sullivan, recalls, "He was serious by nature, but being raised in that environment—the oldest son in a three-person family headed by a single working mother during times of no economic hope—instilled a higher sense of responsibility."

He also became a strong Catholic and attended St. Mary's High School where he was a prominent athlete, quarterback of the football team. He showed forcefulness and leadership acumen early. He earned money for his family as soon as he was able, working part-time jobs at the Marathon plant where his mother was. He would do that every summer, too, eventually using those savings to pay his way through both college and law school. Understanding the paper-making process was bred into him early and deep.

He went to Notre Dame University for undergraduate, where he majored in History, a harbinger of his later interest in everything Civil War. He also squeezed some time in to be a seminarian as part of his Catholic faith. That got short-circuited when he discovered that the priests "wouldn't allow reading of outside materials." He couldn't indulge his insatiable curiosity about the world.

Cementing his Notre Dame connection, he entered its law school. While there, he met his wife-to-be, Rosemary, who was a student at St. Mary's College nearby. He remembered his law school days as "the most stressful of my life," but added that the law study disciplines helped him be effective at separating the important from the unimportant.

He and Rosemary married in 1960 and had a child in 1961. After his law school graduation, he spent a year in the Army while Rosemary and their son went back to live with her parents. Released in 1963, he joined a Milwaukee law firm but soon found out about a corporate counsel opportunity back home in Northeast Wisconsin, at Fort Howard Paper Company, a manufacturing business he already knew well. He was attracted because the Fort Howard story fit him well—cost-conscious, frugal, disciplined, with a "will do" mentality.

He joined the company in 1964, reporting to John Cofrin, the son of CEO/Founder Austin Cofrin. John Cofrin became a mentor to Paul, and when John became CEO in 1970, included Paul closely in all his activities and decision-making. Paul joined the board of the Fort Howard Foundation in 1971 and began administrating it shortly afterwards.

He and Rosemary eventually had five children in the 60s. While free time was at a minimum, he managed to be involved with his kids, who had some of his streaks of athleticism. He coached his oldest son's Bantam hockey team even though he not only had never played hockey, but he also couldn't skate. But he learned fast, was forceful, and the team eventually won the Wisconsin state championship. He was equally involved with his daughters. Susan Sullivan notes, "He made sure I knew how to skate, and he coached our soccer team, which did well, too." He made no distinctions between his sons and daughters, she said. "If you're good, you're good, and should have equal opportunities. You could see that in the way he promoted women when he was at Fort Howard."

His interest in the virtues of wastepaper recycling was also heart-felt. "He would come home at night and read several newspapers that were delivered each day. Then, he'd stack them up until the stack was overflowing, pile them in the car, and take them to the plant to be made into pulp."

Besides Catholic education at all levels, another love was the Civil War. His office at home included a table complete with battlefield mockups and toy soldiers,

"On vacations, he would pile us all into a station wagon, and we'd drive to Florida to see relatives but on the way we'd stop at Civil War battlefields."

and he would regale visitors demonstrating a certain battle's strategies. "On vacations, he would pile us all into a station wagon, and we'd drive to Florida to see relatives but on the way we'd stop at Civil War battlefields."

He remarried in 1985, to Carol.

Unfortunately, his career trajectory was short-circuited in the late 1980s when he was in his early 50s by two heart attacks and a stroke. That resulted in his retirement from Fort Howard. He worked hard to re-train his brain, including using math cards, his family indicates. From then on, his purposeful life focused on overseeing the growth and contributions of the Cornerstone Foundation, the successor to the Fort Howard Foundation, as well as major involvements with the Catholic Diocese in Green Bay, and with Morgan Stanley, the Chicago Federal Reserve Bank, and the Notre Dame Law School.

He died in 2017.

———

John Cofrin, Austin Cofrin's son, joined Fort Howard in 1946, but didn't succeed his father as president until 1960, and though John would die too soon in 1974, his father would continue living until 1980, dying at the age of 97. John was just as frugal and secretive as his father was, but was much more gregarious— a greater "people person." He would hold employee meetings to keep them aware of what was happening and how the company was doing.

He was also irascible. "I flew in from California for the interview," recalls Don DeMeuse of his hiring interview at Fort Howard on a Saturday in 1967, "and was supposed to meet with the HR person, who unexpectedly couldn't be there, so John said to come to his office. When I got there, he just asked, 'Well, do you want the damned job or not?' Later on, when Don wanted to promote a person and John didn't like the idea, John said, 'Well, it's your problem. You'll have to live with him!'" DeMeuse was hired into the Maintenance area, became its supervisor three years later, and almost immediately thereafter, in 1971, was named to lead the Converting group, and in 1975, all manufacturing.

Paul Schierl had been hired earlier as corporate counsel, gradually ingraining himself in the mechanics of understanding how the company operated, which was important because in 1974, upon John's untimely death, Paul took over the company and Don DeMeuse was his most important executive. DeMeuse was special; as an engineer/technician he was excellent at figuring out why machines might not work, and how to make them work faster and better. And he easily created relationships with people at all levels, so was well liked, very respected, and made things happen. He was a company man.

For years as a private company, Fort Howard had just a few shareholders, with Austin as the largest. But as the company did well, some of those shareholders wanted to cash out, so John Cofrin made the difficult decision to create a public offering of stock in order to get funds to buy those shareholders out; others stayed in. The company became listed on the New York Stock Exchange. Now, John had to issue quarterly earnings reports and hold public annual meetings, which he continued to do until management and Morgan Stanley took it private in 1988.

THE Point Of Difference

Mike Riordan, who joined the company in 1983 and became CEO in 1996, says, "We were all about the de-inking technology. We had extraordinary expertise in efficiently applying this technology, allowing us to move towards 100% recycled paper waste, which was a major cost benefit compared to competitors. We knew how to operate huge paper machines to maximum efficiency. That was our expertise—the expertise on which the company was founded. From there, we produced good paper products that competed favorably in the marketplace."

"We were known as a great place to be employed," continues Riordan. "People were urged to apply with us to see if they could get in. We appreciated performance and rewarded it. That kept us non-union, in a city full of unionized paper mills."

"We were also secretive because we knew that this expertise created our competitive dominance. We created a culture and practices to exclude conversations in the community and industry about how we did what we did." Former CFO Jim Schoshinski adds, "They wouldn't even let me join the accountant's association."

"We were known as a great place to be employed," continues Riordan. "People were urged to apply with us to see if they could get in. We appreciated performance and rewarded it. That kept us non-union, in a city full of unionized paper mills."

Also helping was the annual Goodwill Bonus. It was distributed in equal percentage amounts to every employee.

Muskogee was Paul's Boldest Decision

Paul had a challenge that the Cofrins didn't, at least in degree. He had to grow the business because the stock was now publicly listed. DeMeuse, along with others, commented, "He invested in the business, and we could do that without debt because of our large margins and profit." He would continue adding very costly, state-of-the-art paper-making machines to the core Green Bay plant.

In addition, as the Green Bay plant reached capacity, he began exploring doing something the company had never considered before: establishing a second plant. Eventually, they settled on building the plant in Muskogee, Oklahoma, from which they could service the southern and western markets, "saving tens of millions of dollars in trucking costs," says DeMeuse. It was

Kathy Hempel

a close-to- $500 million investment, but also gained the company more than $250 million in revenues each year at the hefty profit margins the company was earning. Starting the plant from scratch, they were able to instill a culture of frugality similar to Green Bay's. It was an extension of Austin Cofrin.

Most executives of that era felt like EVP Kathy Hempel, who stated, "It was Paul's boldest decision, a breakout for the company. It also drove the need for greater professionalization in everything we did—more rigorous processes and procedures for marketing and sales, for finance, HR and public affairs. It drove us to more sophisticated financial analyses, more expert staff members, more training initiatives, more formalized salary structures. Now, government relations became a critical part of the business as we needed to satisfy the regulations of another state as well as more stringent EPA and state environmental requirements."

Transportation And Logistics Excellence

It also drove the company to sophisticate its transportation system by injecting greater professionalism into how it scheduled tractors and trailers to greater efficiency. Fort Howard attracted and developed extraordinary talent to this division and began developing sophisticated software systems to drive daily decisions. It began to become an expert in logistics, developing algorithmic software that delineated the most efficient routes and timing for loads, pickups and backhauls. Indeed, when James River purchased the business in 1997, they thought so much of its expertise that they made the Fort Howard organization the logistics lead for the entire company.

That happened again when Georgia Pacific purchased Fort James in 2003, moving its Atlanta logistics leadership to Green Bay and creating a separate organization.

And when giant Koch Industries purchased GP in 2005, they moved the Koch logistics leadership to Green Bay as well. Called KBX, it now coordinates the logistics of a $115 billion global enterprise from Green Bay.

Paul was doing pre-emptive investments, buying major paper-making machines and new types of specialized converting equipment that gave us features that competitors didn't, which would slow their entry into those offerings."

Going Forward

The company continued to prosper. In 1981, Schierl hired George Hartmann, a marketing and sales guru who had been with larger organizations, as the new VP/Marketing & Sales, with instructions to "sell the capacity with higher margins." George was with another Green Bay company, "but it wasn't investing in expansion, and Fort Howard was. Paul was doing pre-emptive investments, buying major paper-making machines and new types of specialized converting equipment that gave us features

George Hartmann

that competitors didn't, which would slow their entry into those offerings."

They then began sophisticating the R&D and market analysis capabilities to drive more new product innovations. They also made the innovative move of providing napkin, towel, and tissue dispensers free to distributors to give to customers for the Fort Howard products. As an example of backwards integration that yields cost savings, after many years of outsourcing the building of these dispensers, they found room in the machining department and began making them themselves.

Soon, senior management would be distracted, but the basic tissue business and initiatives of the legacy business, and its tremendous low-cost point-of-difference due to its wastepaper and de- inking/recycling capabilities, would continue unabated.

(Indeed, when all the chaos surrounding the business from 1983 when Maryland Cup was purchased, through the 1988 Leveraged Buyout, to the sale of the Cup Division in 1989 ... came to a close, the legacy business would continue to shine, and would be embraced and invested in by both James River as it became Fort James, and by Georgia Pacific when it purchased Fort James. Hartmann points out that when he joined in 1981, Fort Howard had 24% of the Away-From-Home tissue product business in the U.S., under James River it increased to 34%, and under GP it had 40%!)

Before Maryland Cup

The purchase of much larger Maryland Cup in 1983, possible because of its low stock price, wasn't the first attempt into this market. Tim Reilly, a former sales executive with International Paper who joined Fort Howard in 1978 as Marketing Manager to help with the fledging consumer brand business, recalls, "My boss, John Cokins, the Sales VP, showed up at my house one Saturday and asked me to tackle a special project, analyzing whether we should join with a Chicago cup company. It was a big deal, with attorneys involved. In the end, it looked like the deal was not to buy the business, but only the assets,

the production capabilities. That wasn't going to work, and the negotiations fell through."

"It was a major project for me," he continued, "with lots of moving parts to analyze. Finally, I asked to call a meeting of all those I needed to be involved and began handing out assignments. I was giving assignments to people much higher in the organization than me, like Don DeMeuse, the president. With each assignment, I asked, 'Will you commit to doing this?' Everyone

Tim Reilly

said Yes and everyone carried through. That was an essence of the Fort Howard culture. If people said they'd do it, they would."

"Only a week after the completion of that project," Reilly explains, "Paul called me in and gave me another assignment. He explained how the various pieces of the process weren't functioning well together; they weren't talking to each other. As an example, the tissue business was our biggest piece, so it would get priority with shipping, but in the consumer business, I had commitments for delivery dates to our grocery customers to meet their promotion plans, and I needed priority also. We needed shipping to balance these. So, I became an expert in logistics, eventually pulling together a system where everyone's daily needs were being considered and planned for by those who needed to. We called it Operations Planning & Control. At the same time, we were working with IBM to develop a broad-based system for Customer Service, which I was heavily involved in. So, I was coordinating the consumer business, the OPC system (re-named Distribution Services), and the computerization of Customer Service. We also began moving from heavy reliance on shipping by rail to shipping by truckload, which was quicker but costlier."

"By paying attention to the Consumer side," Reilly concludes, "and planning growth, we were growing at the rate of 30% per year and more, which made these logistics improvements ever more critical and necessary. As we planned the new Savannah mill, a lot of it was devoted to producing our consumer brands, mostly for the Southeast markets."

Fort Howard's Culture

While culture is certainly composed of many habitual behaviors, those listed below—all begun under the leadership of Austin Cofrin—stand out the most:

Egalitarian

"There are no executive perks. Even when I had Fort Howard as a customer and visited them, I couldn't take them to lunch; we went to the company cafeteria. There was no favoritism in our social events, either. My golf league partner was from the maintenance department. Same for the bowling league."

Cost Fanatical

"We were paranoid on costs. Maybe too paranoid."

Perform

"We do what we commit to. We get the job done. High expectations."

Secretive

"Our processes, especially on our cost-lowering de-inking and recycled paper processing capabilities, are our competitive differentiator. We don't want anyone to understand them. We don't want outsiders inside our plant if possible."

Take Care Of Your Own

"We are a family. Emulate that as much as possible. Pay decently, and reward when the company does well (Goodwill Bonuses!). Have a No Layoff policy, which means employees get cross-trained so when they run out of work in one area, they can easily move to another."

Over-riding all, of course, was the fanatical focus on cost efficiency, which drove all decisions, including constant capital investments in upgrading and adding the most efficient paper-making machines in the industry. At one point, between its three plants, Fort Howard operated 13 of the 14 most efficient ones in the world.

It showed up in constant improvement in operating practices as well. DeMeuse notes, "The Quality movement in the early 80s was very important to us. It opened our eyes to what was even more possible; we sent a lot of people to train in Chicago. We also got into robotics early, starting with simple functions like picking up and placing napkin cartons as part of the production process and in packing." As pointed out elsewhere, wherever Fort Howard could, DeMeuse says, "We would figure out how to do it ourselves. We were very vertically integrated, very little outsourcing."

Management Techniques
Weekly Senior Management and One-on-One Meetings With Direct Reports

"Paul did lots of reading and thinking on weekends, resulting in energized Monday senior management meetings. He was primed to ask lots of questions about what the data showed, about personnel challenges, everything."

Monthly Blue Book Meeting of the Leadership Team
"The Blue Book was an inch thick with every measurement we had for everything we did the prior month, with projections. As pyramid heads, we had to know our business thoroughly, to the last dime—because Paul did. But I gotta tell you, I never saw a better cost accounting and control system than the one we had."

Monthly Anniversary Celebrations in Room 310
"Not to be missed by leadership. We honored employees reaching their First, Fifth, Tenth, Fifteenth, etc., work anniversaries. We'd have 12-14 in the room, give out awards, eat some cake, but most importantly hear from them what they were thinking about the company and how they are treated, and for us to tell them what was happening with the company overall."

Visiting the Production Floor
"Also, for several years, Paul required all executives to spend one night a month on the production floor, a way to connect with those on the second- and third-shifts. We were asked to write up our observations."

Entering The Cup Business in 1983

"The rationale behind this was that we shared major customers," explains Don Demeuse. "For example, we supplied McDonald's with all their napkins and some non-consumer paper products, and Maryland Cup supplied their disposable plastic plates and cups. They were a good company, and the timing was good because they weren't doing well, their bottom line was low, making the price affordable. Also, their weaknesses were our strengths: Their plants had old, inefficient machinery, their metrics weren't backed with good accounting, and procedures weren't well documented."

What Fort Howard got, with 3,000 employees and two plants, was a company with 10,000 employees and 33 plants worldwide.

It also created a culture that was somewhat paternalistic, not numbers-oriented, and customer- oriented rather than production-oriented—a culture that ultimately wouldn't fit well.

It also created a culture that was somewhat paternalistic, not numbers-oriented, and customer- oriented rather than production-oriented—a culture that ultilmately wouldn't fit well. But Fort Howard management didn't know that yet. In addition, sources say, integrating two legacy salesforces selling disparate products didn't go well, and was then compounded later with the Lily Tulip salesforce.

That said, executives point out (in the words of one), "Fort Howard was the best run company in the tissue business, and Maryland Cup was in fact the best run company in the disposable cup, plate and utensil business."

They immediately began planning investments to upgrade equipment in key plants, and build new ones in England and Hong Kong to better service key customers. They began integrating Fort Howard's accounting and reporting systems and assumed that management would manage to the numbers.

Where they could, and there were substantial places, the Fort Howard management began reducing the workforce, including in the marketing and sales areas because they were used to very lean, moderately paid sales structures. Ultimately, close to 6,000 employees were pared.

While this was going on, two other major events were taking place:

First, in 1985, Lily Tulip became available at an affordable price, so Fort Howard purchased it as well. "They had a new product we thought had great potential, the Trophy cup, which had a foam inside for insulation and a smooth, solid plastic outside," recalls DeMeuse.

The Maryland Cup and Lily Tulip investments, and related upgrades, totaled more than $800 million.

Second, a year after that, but with years of management planning time beforehand, the huge new Savannah plant—with its own 300-inch paper-making machine and related converting equipment—opened. A $500 million investment. With the transportation savings, the 30% annual increases in the consumer brands that would be produced there, and the cost efficiencies, everything looked rosy—and it was. The tissue business was on track with capacity to achieve $1 billion in sales.

So, in 1986 and 1987, Paul Schierl is watching his team on two fronts: putting in place the new Savannah plant, but also trying to quickly turn around the new Cup Division behemoth—two different, somewhat dysfunctional organizations with different operating systems, even different systems between their plants.

Part of the Maryland Cup acquisition was Mike Riordan, the HR head of its Sweetheart Cup division in Chicago. He had experience negotiating union contracts at Sweetheart as well as a union decertification. During the due diligence period, Paul spent many hours in Chicago bring briefed by Riordan on what operating a unionized organization was like, and what negotiating with unions was like. That became important later when Lily Tulip, with its four unionized plants, were bought.

He moved Riordan to Baltimore, Maryland Cup's headquarters, ultimately in charge of all Cup Division HR functions and union relationships. He reported to EVP Kathy Hempel in Green Bay.

"It was not an easy time," recalls Mike. "Competition was increasing, and we had to create efficiencies through plant closings. I was actually trying to negotiate wage decreases as one technique to maintain a plant's

Combining two cultures requires serious analysis of people, their inclinations, and behaviors, and we didn't know how to do that.

profitability so it wouldn't be closed, and its business consolidated with another. Over time, we reduced our Cup Division workforce by 6,000, down to 8,000 employees by the time we were sold in 1989."

Don DeMeuse, who spent much of his time with Cup Division challenges, notes, "Our idea was to impose our culture on it, upgrade the manufacturing capability, create a more efficient selling structure increasing the marketplace for both our tissue and paper products, and their drink containers and plates. Combining two cultures requires serious analysis of people, their inclinations, and behaviors, and we didn't know how to do that. And then we compounded the problem by doing the same two years later with Lily Tulip."

Taking Fort Howard Private

In October 1987, there was a stock market crash and all stocks cratered, including Fort Howard. It was $62 per share before the crash and dropped to $32 afterwards, before trending up. Paul worried about a takeover by a larger entity or even a private equity grab. The concept of a Leveraged Buyout wasn't new; indeed, KI had done one several years earlier in Green Bay.

Schierl began talking with Morgan Stanley, the large and well-positioned New York investment bank, about doing the same, and taking Fort Howard private again. Because the rest of the organization was consumed with the Cup Division challenges, he and CFO Kathy Hempel, along with a special committee of independent Board members representing shareholder interests, composed of Thomas Shaffer, a law school professor, and Green Bay businesspeople James Cuene and Paul Ziemer, led the effort to make the deal happen. It included the massive amount of data and projections necessary to explain the deal as well as create confidence that the organization would continue well managed and successful. Don DeMeuse and CFO Jim Schoshinski were also present at some of the meetings.

It was a big deal because Fort Howard was now a very large organization. When the transaction finished in 1988, Morgan Stanley's Morgan Stanley Capital Partners private equity arm became the majority owner of the company.

Explaining The LBO Process

An explanation of the Leveraged Buyout Process, which was utilized by both KI and Fort Howard, with an example, is provided in Appendix I.

Also, as occurs in many ownership changes, some shareholders filed a federal lawsuit questioning the appropriateness of the process as being too narrow in focus to provide a good estimation of share value. The judge's opinion, which vindicated the process used and the appropriateness of the share value, is an excellent review of the process that occurred:

Fort Howard Shareholders Litigation, 9991 (1988); https://casetext.com/case/in-re-fort-howard-shareholders-litigation.

Sadly, for Paul Schierl's career, during the negotiations at the age of 53, he had a small heart attack. Two years later, in 1990, he suffered another one and was taken to Cleveland Clinic for the operation, and while there, had a stroke. That signaled the end of his working career, and he retired from the business.

In the interim, Morgan Stanley had seen enough and sold the entire Cup Division business. Proceeds amounted to $620 million, well below the $868 million invested in it.

Don DeMeuse assumed the CEO position and would run the company as it always had been, but under the watchful eye of Morgan Stanley. Sales now were in the $1.2 billion range, and operating income was $270 million but interest on the debt was a burdensome $423 million.

Morgan Stanley Takes The Company Public Again

In the early 1990s, Morgan Stanley decided to issue public stock again, issuing 37 million shares in 1995-1996 with the proceeds used to retire some of the debt, and began selling off its considerable investment to reduce its share of ownership.

By 1995, sales were $1.6 billion, and the company had 6,800 employees worldwide.

Morgan Stanley began looking for another buyer, eventually finding James River Corp., which would be a good strategic fit for Fort Howard and help James River compete more strongly with Kimberly Clark and P&G. This transaction was for an exchange of stock valued at $3.4 billion, plus assumption of $2.4

billion in debt. James River already had 950 employees in Green Bay, adding to Fort Howard's 3,300.

Don DeMeuse had been with the company since 1967 and was a manufacturing guy—an operator—not at ease with the Morgan Stanley oversight and emphasis on the financial strategies and the continuing interest burden. He retired and Mike Riordan succeeded him as CEO. When the James River transaction occurred, Riordan became president of the combined company, headquartered in Chicago. Riordan wasn't that pleased with the Fort James approaches, either, but committed to making the acquisition work at least for a year. He served "a year and a day."

Another recalls, "James River wasn't run as tightly as we were. When Fort Howard expanded, plants would use the identical cost systems, metrics, and goals. Under James River, each plant seemed to have its own systems and procedures."

For George Hartmann, though, aligning with James River was "like a breath of fresh air. They were a marketing and sales organization, so we became much more sophisticated in how we went to market. My job was 'loved and respected.' We weren't just 'selling capacity.'"

In 2003, Fort James was purchased by Georgia Pacific, based in Atlanta. Two original Fort Howard executives were retained, including Hartmann who became VP over one of GP's biggest divisions.

Environmentalism and the Greenpeace Incident

Fort Howard officials have always said they practice extraordinarily high conformance to environmental regulations, and they have awards and citations to back that up.

Nevertheless, in 1985, the activist environmental group Greenpeace, knowing that the Fox River had been proven to be high in toxic PCB discharges by paper companies and been designated a SuperFund site, was dedicated to raising the visibility of that danger. They sailed a ship into Green Bay's harbor and publicized their desire to expose Fort Howard.

In anticipation, Fort Howard strung a fence across the riverbank and posted guards. Greenpeace divers found out that the plant had three discharge pipes into the river but had only reported one and ultimately made that a public issue. They took samples of the effluent to show the PCB discharge, but the sample analyses showed the company was well within range of all guidelines. One executive noted, "Our goal was to process the water, so it was cleaner when we released it than when we took it in."

Schierl, who was a strong advocate of Fort Howard's secrecy, admitted, "Greenpeace brought to the forefront the fact that we haven't been handling our community relations as well as we should have been."

A few years later, the company hired Cliff Bowers, a respected local communications expert, to handle their outside public relations, a sign of the trend towards greater open-ness. "I benefited from the mellowing that the Greenpeace incident caused."

More About Paul Schierl

• "His Why: To dominate! He would do pre-emptive investing. If he heard a competitor was considering something, and it seemed strategically right, he would get into it faster and slow the competitor."

• " He was extremely smart. Insightful analysis and making good decisions were his strengths. But collective decision-making was not part of his makeup. He didn't involve others well in obtaining information relative to making decisions. He had a strong streak of autocracy in him. Like some leaders with this tendency, he could periodically exaggerate the problem or opportunity."

• "He loved the challenges of business, the strategy, the commitment to build a lasting organization."

• " He had a very strategic mind, and was able to consider bold, new strategies ... like Muskogee, Savannah and the LBO, and also relished the normal challenges in the daily give-and-take with customers and suppliers."

• "Like many good leaders, he wouldn't penalize people for disagreement but would rather embrace it ... but without indicating he appreciated it."

• "He was serious, not fun. If you performed, you were in his good graces, and he took care of you. If you didn't, he would have the conversation with you."

- "Because he didn't care what others thought, he could call a spade a spade and become a thorn in the side of other community leaders whom he didn't think were making decisions to the community's benefit."

- "For Paul, sales and marketing was a downer. He was bad at schmoozing."

- He really appreciated Green Bay's work ethic, and the employees who made up the Fort Howard family who emulated it. "We would work six days a week, and ten hours a day, and think nothing of it. Just the way it was. He did the same."

- "He was brutal in staff meetings."

- "Our chemistry as a senior organization was extremely unique. We all had a sense of working together for the common good. Yes, we had disagreements, but once a decision was made, we worked together to make it happen. Don DeMeuse was a critical component in all of this."

- "Like many leaders with rough edges, he also had a soft heart that wasn't often visible to most. I've seen him in tears when dealing with an employee who had a need. His compassion could be very high."

- "His loves outside his work were Notre Dame ... and the Fort Howard Foundation. That's where he could do good within the community."

- Another love, in his retirement, was his friendship with young Nick Hafeman, to whom he was a Big Brother as part of Big Brothers Big Sisters.

Dick Resch

We are grateful to the following current and former executives for their insights which created this chapter:
Mike Carmichael
Brian Krenke
Mark Olsen
Amy Perrault
Bob Pyle
Beth Relich
Dick and Sharon Resch
Dan Schiltz
Beth Seymour
Marty Wikoff

Green Bay's Golden Age:
Dick Resch
KI

"If you have skin in the game, you will perform much more strongly."
~Dick Resch

The Short Version

In 1964, when Dick Resch joined Krueger Metals as a 25-year-old, A.F. Krueger's company was a 50-employee, $4 million manufacturer of metal folding chairs and, in a brand-new Tupelo, MS, plant, folding tables.

When Dick and the management team, via one of the nation's earliest Leveraged Buy-Outs, took over from Phil Hendrickson in 1982, the company did about $50 million and was already beginning to grow more quickly. When he retired in 2019, after 38 years as CEO and 55 years as an employee, KI was doing $600 million in volume, with 1800 employees and 8 plants, and was or had been the primary supplier of office furniture to organizations like Microsoft, Google and Facebook.

That LBO left Northwestern Mutual as the 51% owner of the business, but fast, profitable growth allowed Dick in 1986 to initiate another buyout that removed Northwestern Mutual entirely and significantly increased the percentage owned by 75 members of the management team (and with significant bank debt).

Marketplace Innovations

By 1983, the company was already engaging in market differentiation practices to make it more effective against the billion-dollar competitors like Steelcase, Hon, Herman Miller and Hayworth. The main initiative was to market cutting-edge furniture designs. The first was a desk chair providing unique ergonomic support, called Vertebra, designed by Italian designer Giancarlo Piretti. That began getting Krueger noticed in the marketplace.

Dick was also reaching out to major thinkers in the brand management and Go-To-Market worlds, especially Rowland Moriarty of Harvard Business School. Between them, they designed a vertical market approach that created five Business Units, each with its own marketing and selling organizations: Education K-12 continued to be sold through existing dealers, but they would approach the College/University market with direct selling, as they would Health Care and Large Businesses.

The fifth major initiative for Krueger was to serve the huge Government facilities market. It wasn't a market that the giants in the industry wanted to play in, because it first starts with Prisons. When Krueger would win a bid, it would provide kits of the products to a prison where prisoners would do the assembly work. Then, Krueger might also have the contract to oversee installation. This "Prison" market at one point became a full third of revenues, and two-thirds of operating income—very significant, and an important stable base from which to initiate risky innovations in other markets.

Plant-Based Innovations

In the 1990s, Dick became intrigued by the idea of Market-of-One, based on a book by Don Pepper and Martha Rodgers, where you treated each order uniquely. When efficiencies are achieved through continuous flow manufacturing, it's a huge burden on the production processes because you must treat each order as its own batch and renounce those assembly-line efficiencies. But initiating cell manufacturing softened that negative, and it worked tremendously as a customer- acquisition differentiator.

An immediate success was getting the prestigious Microsoft business. When Microsoft added an employee, a coder or a programmer, that employee might need a unique cubicle configuration. Krueger, soon becoming KI, had two people at the Microsoft headquarters in Bellevue, WA, who would lay out that cubicle and fax the design to the Green Bay plant, where it would be planned, scheduled, assembled, packed, and shipped within a week. That meant eliminating assembly lines and creating "Cells" of 5-6 employees, called technicians, who were cross trained in most of the production skills needed, and who would do their own assigning and changing of responsibilities to ensure their workload was accomplished on schedule. If they were successful, it meant more money in their paycheck based on a plant-based Gain- Sharing plan that took into consideration On-Time Shipping, Re-Work, and other performance indicators.

As the Quality movement gained traction, KI was implementing those features as well, which also reduced cost and increased speed.

Dick was very amenable to testing any effort that looked like it would improve the production process. He even employed a young Ph.D., Marty Wikoff, who was associated with a team of behavioral scientists from Notre Dame, and they carried out tests and implementations of "soft skills" that would better assure

Marty Wikoff

engagement and morale. Things as simple as charting production and providing positive reinforcement, and having technicians evaluate their supervisors on how often and well they did it. Wikoff also did studies of salespeople and how they did their jobs and made changes in the sales processes as a result.

On Wellness

Wikoff was also appointed head of Human Resources at one point, and had responsibility for oversight of KI's Wellness program, which already included a cutting-edge element of tying employees Health Risk Assessment scores to the health insurance premium they were charged a decade before this became common. KI invested in a substantial fitness equipment room and supported healthy events such as runs.

A physical activity devotee, Dick was a runner for many years, and later a cyclist and kayaker. Here he is with KI employees who won trophies at a convention-sponsored event.

The 100% ESOP

Dick many times over the years told his fellow management team members that he wanted KI headquarters

to stay in Green Bay and wanted to support the community. He was aware that when a company headquarters leaves the area, that much community involvement by managers and employees, as well as monetary contributions, are significantly reduced.
"I want to invest my money back into the community that helped me make it," he told people.

He was aware that when a company headquarters leaves the area, that much community involvement by managers and employees, as well as monetary contributions, are significantly reduced.

But Dick was by far the major shareholder, and to buy him out would not be easy. Three times he went through exercises to look at an outsider buyer who would commit to keeping KI local, or at how to sell to the management team, which turned out to be prohibitively expensive. Finally, in 2018, he reached agreement with banks to fund a 100% ESOP, which would buy him out over five years, and leave all employees as shareholders, whose share values would increase as the debt was paid down.

Management Transition

It's tough for a CEO to relinquish responsibility, especially after 36 years. It's your baby, and it's a big baby! But now Brian Krenke, a trusted 20+-year member of the KI Team, who came up through the sales ranks, has the responsibility of being CEO, reporting to an outside board even though it's a private company. He oversees a management team that also has significant tenure, so the transition is relatively seamless.

Brian Krenke

Early Years

Dick was born in 1938 in Grand Forks, North Dakota, where his mom and dad were both teachers. The family lived frugally and saved their dollars, and eventually his father found a better- paying job in Minneapolis as an advertising copy writer, so the family moved there. During his growing up years, Dick managed three newspaper routes to make money, with not much time for anything else other than participating in YMCA programs. One summer, he was asked to be the leader of several of the YMCA camp counselors; he says that that experience was key in helping him understand much of the responsibilities, opportunities, and techniques of leadership that he would practice much later. At Central High School, he was academically focused, and graduated #8 in a large senior class; #1 was a girl named Sharon James. (Much later, Dick would attend a high school reunion, meet Sharon James again, and they would get married. Sharon herself has become a major force in community activities in Green Bay.)

His parents had met at Graceland College, then a two-year, fairly strict (no drinking or smoking) liberal arts institution affiliated with the Reorganized Church of Latter-Day Saints, and after Dick graduated high school in 1956, he went there. His main contribution remembered by the college was a prank, when he and his best friend climbed a local building and painted the top black.

He was interested in engineering and decided to apply to and was accepted at MIT in Cambridge, MA, where he studied mechanical engineering and participated for three years on the university's lightweight division rowing team, which daily consumed three hours or more during the season. From MIT, he applied to Harvard Business School, just down the street in Cambridge, was accepted, and spent two years in their case study curriculum as a finance major, graduating in 1963.

Now, he needed a real job. "I had no particular interest; I just needed a job!" he recalled. He joined Hudson Pulp & Paper Co., partially because it was headquartered in New York City. His assignments were to visit the company's various paper mills and critique them according to certain guidelines. But Hudson, eventually acquired by Georgia-Pacific, was owned, and managed by a tight family dynasty, so prospects for advancement were slim, and now married with a child, he and his wife, Nancy, were ready to move back to the Midwest.

Through a friend-of-a-friend, he heard of an opening at the small furniture company in Green Bay, went there to interview with A.F. Krueger, the owner, and joined, starting as Krueger's assistant-in-training in 1964, the same year that Krueger set up a remote plant in less-costly Tupelo, Mississippi. At the time, they were an industry-dominating company making metal folding chairs and a variety of folding tables, selling to both commercial and institutional customers.

"We were a team of just 7-8 leaders for the next decade or more, doing our best to grow the company and stay profitable." In 1967, A.F. died, and second-in-command Phil Hendrickson took over the company. Dick's involvements were primarily working on sophisticating manufacturing processes, as VP/Manufacturing from 1967 to 1975.

Hendrickson promoted him to EVP in1975, and Dick became more involved in stimulating growth and ownership concentration in management.

The Path To Growth

Originally, Krueger Manufacturing was located on West Mason St., approximately where LaForce Hardware is now. They didn't move to the Bellevue location until 1978. The company was not inconsequential during the early 1970's, growing to more than $30 million during that decade and requiring the Bellevue expansion. It operated the

The Krueger Metals office and plant on West Mason St.

low-cost Tupelo plant making folding tables and had a mail order marketing operation in Milwaukee and New York. It was making and selling tens of thousands of folding tables and chairs.

Two major initiatives during the 1970s, in addition to Dick's rise as an operations efficiency guru, reflected his broad interests in having an energizing workplace and taking on much larger competitors.

One was the initiation, along with owner Phil Hendrickson, of bringing in a Milwaukee company, Heath, to analyze the company's financial and operating stats in detail, very quickly after the end of each month, and then making a presentation to the management group on what they were seeing, for good and ill.

Phil and Dick would create conversations around the trends and other findings. This was where Dick nurtured the culture of quick reactions to negative trends. (The Heath presentations would continue for more than 40 years, although today they constitute 650 charts via computer; they're now being modified to project forward as well as historically. About 35 managers attend, and as the Heath facilitator makes points, the relevant operating manager provides additional insight.)

The other was experimenting with more differentiated furniture for the commercial office market, a major step up from folding chairs and tables.

The other was experimenting with more differentiated furniture for the commercial office market, a major step up from folding chairs and tables. They engaged an Italian designer, Giancarlo Piretti, who designed the first desk chair that provided ergonomic support, a bow to the emerging interest in that challenge. It was called the Vertebra, and they introduced it at industry conferences, getting raves for its innovation. They began to be noticed.

They opened a plant in Treviso, Italy, producing goods for customers there and in the U.S., especially using designs created by another Italian furniture maker, Castelli.

In 1982, Dick took over as CEO when Phil Hendrickson retired, and the growth process began to gel and accelerate.

KI began innovating either by being very early in a process or by creating a wholly new idea.

In the mid-1980s, desktop computer systems began emerging, and KI was early in this movement with its COM System, designed in Italy, which hid all those wires.

As workers wanted individual workspaces, KI introduced wall panel systems adaptable for small work groups as well as individuals. They created their own line of ergonomic computer workstations, with all sorts of adjustment features.

To accommodate the growth, Dick began adding

The main KI plant in Green Bay

plants, first in Manitowoc, WI, in 1988, for walls and computer furniture, expanded two years later. Then, they created Pallas Textiles to design and market artistic fabrics. The Gillett plant was moved to Bonduel in 1992.

Sales were almost $180 million by 1990, and employment was more than 1,000.

Innovation Doesn't Stop

On one hand, KI's competitors for the corporate market were the biggest furniture makers in the U.S.—Steelcase, Herman Miller, Hon and Hayworth, all in the billions and multi-billions category. On the other hand, through design and relationships/service, you could position yourself separately in the marketplace.

So, innovation continued, often through purchase.

In the 1990s, a renovated Pembroke, Canada plant began providing designer filing cabinets and other products. Uniquely, Pembroke products began being purchased by Microsoft, Sun Microsystems, and by Office Depot for the smaller office market.

The Perry Stackable Chair won international media attention, as did the Versa chair.

KI acquired AGI Industries of High Point, NC, for its tables and soft lounge seating, especially for the healthcare market. And Period Furniture of Henderson, KY, for its solid wood furniture for the college dormitories and government housing markets.

Its largest acquisition was Spacesaver Corp., Fort Atkinson, WI, which made rolling, collapsible filing systems—perfect for healthcare, offices, libraries and museums that store something for a long time.

At this point, the open space concept was emerging, and ergonomics was becoming even bigger. KI's design teams worked to develop new approaches to these needs, with an emphasis on flexibility and re-use.

In 1997, revenues hit $500 million, and employment over 2,500.

In 1998, one of their furniture designs, its Flexible Workspace line, won the industry's highest award as Best of Competition.

For the education market, KI designed its Einstein brand, later re-named Intellect due to copyright challenges.

Other design innovations continued to come: Genius walls for schools. Spacesaver's Designer Series in the files/storage category, and its Silver Award for its TouchPad Release system for security. Pallas' new Alloy panel fabric. The imaginative lectern for the Wharton business school. The Piretti Dance Chair. AGI's Grand Salon lounge furniture.

The 1981 and 1986 LBO's

Founder AF Krueger passed away in the late 1970s, and his heirs wanted to sell their stock. To facilitate that, Dick suggested to Phil that they use a new technique called a Leveraged Buyout, leveraged in the sense that they would utilize lots of "other people's money." What was fashioned was that Northwestern Mutual Life would own 51% of the shares, and Dick and seven others the rest, with three banks, M&I, Kellogg Green Bay (now Associated Bancorp) and First Wisconsin providing $30 million in debt at 15% interest. Remember, these were very high interest rate years. Says one executive, "Dick took a hell of a risk. This was a monumental undertaking." Phil Hendrickson would exit the company with his share of the buyout, and Dick became CEO. Jack Puelicher, M&I CEO, was the critical partner in the deal, and maintained Dick's gratitude for years.

Growth in profitability continued to happen and the debt continued to decrease, so in 1986 Dick made a move to re-finance and take Northwestern Mutual out, yielding much more of the ownership to an additional 75 managers. The same banks participated, and a private placement with Prudential occurred. The 75 additional shareholders had to ante the then going value of a share, and they did with confidence in the track of the organization.

Mark Olsen, later CFO, recalls, "Dick didn't have to do that. But he felt strongly that if you have skin in the game, you will perform much stronger. It's true. I became an owner at that point and found that I worked a whole lot differently than when I wasn't an owner. The same hours, but

I became an owner at that point and found that I worked a whole lot differently than when I wasn't an owner. The same hours, but something was different and better. We learned more about work ethic and how to work together.

something was different and better. We learned more about work ethic and how to work together."

The 1984-1985 Strike

An executive from the time, recalls, "Krueger Metals was a union shop, but not a strong one. Dick had taken over the CEO role, and we were in the midst of a lot of change in how we approached the customer—more independent decision-making, faster turnaround, things we needed to be doing to beat out the much bigger competitors and make a difference to get business from major customers. All that had ramifications in the production process. It required flexibility in work rules, which during the negotiation process the union leaders, who were outside the company, didn't want to change sufficiently. Ultimately, the result was a strike. It lasted several months."

"The union" he continued, "brought in people from other companies who were very intimidating even to our employee strikers. Some of our employees did cross the picket line, and some paid the price for it. I paid a price with a brick through a window of my home. Many office workers would come down and work on the plant floor at night after their regular work shift. We did hire replacements, who were intimidated, too. Finally, the striking employees decertified the union. We kept the replacements who were good workers, and gradually brought back the strikers. Ultimately, because of our growth, all were offered jobs again."

Market Of One and Cell Manufacturing

Dick was a reader, and one of the books that influenced him in 1993 was The One-To-One Future, by Don Pepper and Martha Rogers. It discussed the idea of going even narrower than being market-focused by being customer-focused and customizing products for each customer. Dick interpreted it even narrower, to customers within the customer.

Microsoft and Sun Microsystems were both huge, fast-growing tech companies, and were adding people ... and offices/cubicles ... at a rapid rate, each of which needed slightly different configurations to meet the specific work needs of the occupant. No other competitor was thinking about that.

To do it and make it a differentiating selling point, KI's manufacturing had to be organized not for fast assembly-line production, but for customized, job-shop-like work. That meant incorporating a new concept called cellular manufacturing, where employees didn't do just one function, but were grouped in small cells where everyone was cross-trained for each function and could apply it on an as-needed basis as an order flowed through the cell.

It requires great coordination, because the drawing of the cubicle had to be sent overnight by fax (and eventually by computer), then the requirements entered via CadCam capability to direct machines to make each part (and then finish it with the right coating) before all parts came together in the cell for assembly. The plant floor had to be good at all of this.

Plus, they wanted speed. If the new employee at Microsoft was arriving on Monday, the prior Monday the KI representative on-site at Microsoft would draw the plans, fax them overnight, entry was the next day—final assembly of the shipment package within two days—shipping to Microsoft for assembly in the cubicle as the employee was being oriented. Or very close!

All this created a significant differentiator from competitors, especially the big ones, and KI took advantage of it, not only with other tech companies, but any growing company with major office expansion needs.

As one KI manager opined, "This was sheer genius. It propelled us to the fastest-growing company in the industry. Basically, we would provide furniture customized for a specific office or cubicle. No one else could do that. No one else had that flexibility. It gave us a major beat in the marketplace. It also required a revolutionary change in how we operated in manufacturing."

Relich, now KI's VP/HR, continues, "I remember working on a special desk for an Ohio school which eventually became a standard product for us, the Dorsal Student Desk. We also created a customized classroom teacher's podium for Wharton Business School that became a standard product as well, the Wharton Lectern."

Bob Pyle

On Microsoft

You're wondering how an upstart Green Bay company collared mammoth Microsoft in 1995 as its primary furniture provider. Here's the words of Bob Pyle, a ten-year KI office systems leader at the time: "Microsoft put out an RFP for their business, and all the Bigs plus us showed interest. We all attended their explanation sessions in Bellevue and, lo and behold, all the Bigs said they had just the right looks already in their offerings. We went back to our Manitowoc plant, where the furniture might be made, got the design group together for several weeks, and developed a panel/furniture system based on what they told us they were looking for. We shipped it to the Microsoft headquarters and assembled it for review. That kicked off extended discussion about the changes desired in our designs, as well as parallel talks with the Bigs.

"I can't promise you we're getting the business, but I need you and Dick here in Bellevue at 10 AM tomorrow!"

"Then, at 8 PM one evening, I got a call from our salesperson saying, 'I can't promise you we're getting the business, but I need you and Dick here in Bellevue at 10 AM tomorrow!' I called Dick and told him. We couldn't get there by 10 AM, but we arrived at 2 PM.

"Of interest: Bill Gates required that his office be outfitted first, so he knew what everyone would be experiencing."

"We did meet with them and walked away with an initial $25 million contract! Over the next two years, we oversaw the complete re-outfitting of the Microsoft headquarters organization and supplied everything they needed as they continued to expand. Eventually, it was worth $100 million to KI.

"Of interest: Bill Gates required that his office be outfitted first, so he knew what everyone would be experiencing."

Setting Up Market Leaders

Dick was also reaching out to major thinkers in the brand management and Go-To-Market worlds, especially Rowland Moriarty of Harvard Business School who was also on the board of the big box retailer, Home Depot. Between them, they designed a vertical market approach that created five Business Units, each with its own marketing and selling organizations: Education K-12 continued to be sold through dealers, but they would approach the

Dan Schiltz

College/University market with **direct selling**, as they would Health Care and Large Businesses. This drove the growth breakthrough for KI.

It didn't happen all at once; it evolved. One executive recalls, "When we work through dealers, we're just one of several product books on their shelves. Dick's idea of breaking away from the dominant channel was genius for us. It differentiated us from the Billionaire competitors. We could directly sell the benefits of our customized, Market-of-One approach which says we're going to provide what you want, not

what's in our product catalogue. We were already very relationship-oriented, so the customer attention we provided was right in our wheelhouse."

The fifth market, which Dick targeted in 1988, was highly unusual and very lucrative: the huge government facilities market. You bid to the federal government purchasing agency, called Unicor. Because it might compromise their brand, the Bigs didn't play here. It starts with Prisons. When Krueger would win a bid, it would provide the parts of the products to a prison where prisoners were paid to do the assembly work (and in many prisons, actual manufacturing using high-end machinery). Then, Krueger might or might not oversee installation, but could also make money on other parts of the enterprise, such as engineering or transportation. Government facilities are not required to buy through the prison

"Until now, we were an engineering company, driven to manufacture as cost efficiently as possible. To Dick's credit, he changed and in 24 months moved us to a market-focused point of view."

enterprises though, so those enterprises also have their own selling organizations. In some cases, KI would even provide the salesforce.

Now, KI sells to the prison enterprises in 45 of the 50 states, as well as the federal government. Called Original Equipment

Industries within Krueger, at one point it provided two-thirds of operating income on barely one-third of revenues. Government spending is subject to the vagaries of federal and state budgets.

Mike Carmichael

At its peak, KI's revenues were $150 million from this market; today about $120 million.

Bob Pyle, who ran the Office Systems initiative recalls, "Until now, we were an engineering company, driven to manufacture as cost efficiently as possible. To Dick's credit, he changed and in 24 months moved us to a market-focused point of view. The engineers would tell us to lower the arms or do something else to make the piece cheaper to manufacture, and Dick would say, 'You don't get it yet. We have to manufacture what the market is telling us they will buy!'"

Meshing going directly to major players, selling the Market-of-One concept, while segregating by specific marketplaces, wasn't a quick execute. It takes time for salespeople to adapt to the new approach. And creative sales management. Mike Carmichael became sales manager about the start of the initiative. "In our piece of the business, we were selling about $1 million a month. We told the salespeople we would hold a party every month we beat the prior month. We had parties each of the first three months. So, we upped it to a party only if the previous month was exceeded by $1 million. We had five more months of those parties."

"We didn't get our growth just by adding salespeople," he continued. "Much of it was by getting better and smarter. It's actually easier to sell directly to large companies. They know what they're doing and what they want. We took the stance that we are helping them. Our approach became High Service/High Relationships."

Today, KI is the largest furniture player in the U.S. in the Education K-12, College/University and Prison marketplaces.

Sophisticating Selling Approaches

Working with Marty Wikoff, Dick began to sophisticate the selling processes, developing techniques that today are commonplace but 30 years ago were ground-breaking. "Until then, hiring salespeople was based on good guesses. So, we began examining the differences between high, average and low performers and understanding their characteristics, and then building those into the hiring process.

Product Modification Niche

A direct result of this approach is that KI created a market niche of Product Modification. "We would adapt the design of a chair or table or office system to what the user would want. That meant the software system had to be able to efficiently design that, communicate it in terms of parts forming, program the machines to do that forming, and schedule it within a cell. All almost immediately," recalls Beth Relich, a manufacturing support person at the time.

A special "cell" that eventually became a department was created within the office, providing the service of adapting product configurations to meet specific customers' needs. They named the service, Infinity.

"We were moving to more sophisticated sales skills requirements as we moved from selling institutional furniture (tables and chairs) to high design, high impact furniture systems, from selling to buyers to selling to architects. Our sales cycles were becoming longer, and we needed a sales process with more stage-gates in it, not to mention a commensurate training and measurement process. We felt that Neil Rackham, later of Spin Selling fame, had developed processes based on behavioral analyses, so we brought him in as our consultant.

"Before, salespeople would estimate where they were in the pipeline for a particular prospect, just wishful guesses, usually way off. We defined each stage-gate in descriptive terms, so we and they could have more disciplined information for planning. We kept analyzing a sales manager's needs and the salesperson's needs, and developed a slew of other analytical programs, such as Sales Optimization, Major Account Analysis, and the like. We achieved a reputation in the industry for having one of the best salesperson development programs. We had programs salespeople could attend only if they had completed pre-requisites. Sometimes, sales managers would ask to have a salesperson attend because 'he knows most of that intuitively.' Dick would have none of that. Accountability. You had to have the prerequisites. If you didn't, the guidelines would be diluted and be of no value. You couldn't be sure what a person knew and didn't know."

In-Plant Innovations

The move to Cellular Manufacturing not only supported the Market-of-One differentiator with competitors, as mentioned it also required a revolutionary change in how manufacturing worked. It was a big change. Explains one-time Manufacturing Supply Chain VP Beth

Beth Seymore

Seymour, "Instead of making the parts of a piece of a furniture in bulk through the batch process, and then using assembly lines to assemble them, because of the needed customization we had cells of 5-6 technicians who operated in a self-directed manner to schedule each other to specific assignments to get done the furniture items that were assigned to the cell. They would huddle each morning to go over the shipping schedule for the next few days, and plan how they would produce the required quantities of each piece. They would make assignments to each other, and to reduce boredom and the likelihood of carpel tunnel, they would exchange roles during each day as well.

"The raw metal to be bent and punched would be delivered to the cell, but the cell technicians would do every needed function except certain very specialized ones like upholstering the seats or operating the chrome baths to put the new surface on the chair or table."

"The Quality movement also had a hand in how everyone checked the prior person's work. There was a robust Quality metric program that included rejects, shortages, re-work, and service repeats. All these were included in a Quality metric the Cell was held for. When we began, our Warranty/Bad Quality outcome was 4% of production; with time, we got it down to the 1% norm people felt you couldn't get below."

"We instituted Lean programs, training people and teams to analyze work processes to improve them. A Suggestion program would provide a token each contributor could use in the vending machines, and at the end of the month, those who contributed the most impactful suggestions received significant rewards, like a canoe for a winner who enjoyed camping.

Every metric that related to what they could control was provided on a real-time basis, including the P&L for the plant. Thus, and this was an objective of Dick's, employees became very facile in what went into determining the bottom-line result.

"Another key element was Metric Transparency. Every metric that related to what they could control was provided on a real-time basis, including the P&L for the plant. Thus, and this was an objective of Dick's, employees became very facile in what went into determining the bottom-line result. And they could financially benefit: Through the Gain-Sharing program based on plant performance, including on-time shipping, quality, and other key measures, they could increase their income by as much as 10% through good performance."

Seymour continued, "Too, there was a Pay For Applied Knowledge program, patterned after that at other companies. It wasn't too complicated, and the technicians understood it well. Because we wanted skill flexibility within the Cells and between functions, we wanted people to know as many jobs as they could, at as high an expertise level as they could. As they got training in various skills, like welding, operating the punch press, painting, injection molding and the like, their hourly pay would increase."

"The result of all of this: High trust levels between technicians, managers and senior executives, and a willingness to do what was needed to get the company's jobs done on time. We became very used to change that would yield improvement."

How Dick Would Embrace Innovation

Beth Relich and a fellow engineer had been exposed to Cellular Manufacturing techniques while at UW-Madison; Dick had read about it. Beth and her partner looked at the Matrix Chair production process, requiring manufacture of 1200-1500 chairs a day, including the plating process where the chrome application occurred. "The inventory was all over the place, and the assembled frames had to be transported significant distances back-and-forth from plating. We analyzed whether it could be done better with the Cellular Manufacturing techniques and laid out a plan. The moves would cost about $10,000. Dick said No. We pressed further, and he finally acquiesced to let us try it."

The outcomes were substantially better than the legacy approach. Inventories of parts declined, space requirements declined, distances traveled declined, quality in terms of bad parts and returns decreased, other costs decreased, morale increased, and on-time completion became more reliable. "Dick reacts well to any improvements, so he gave us a free hand to begin converting other product areas as a result. Over two years, we relayed the entire plant. Eventually, the story became known within the industry, and I began having to give tours. If it was a customer or prospective customer, both Dick and Darryl Jarascewski, the manufacturing leader, would come along on the tours."

Marty Wikoff, The On-Site Ph.D.

"If there was a potential for improving performance, that was Dick's forte," says Wikoff. "He was a devotee of measurements and accountability. Dick heard a presentation by a Notre Dame Productivity Institute head, Chris Anderson, at one of his TEC CEO Group meetings, and was intrigued. Anderson's presentation focused on behavior modification research he was doing, and they created a relationship. Wikoff was a graduate student working with Anderson, and they agreed for Marty to be "hired" into Krueger at $500 per month to begin using manufacturing departments for additional research, beginning in fiberglass, then upholstery, then welding, then plating. Dick's charge to Marty was "To beat the Tupelo plant performance, which is quite good." The first experiments were to develop and post charts and graphs of performance statistics, and then provide regular

Beth Relich

feedback to operators on those results. That move alone increased performance at least 15%. Very rudimentary by today's standards, but cutting edge back in the late 1970's.

The second was to test the efficacy of Positive Reinforcement—to say Thank You for jobs well done. This also cemented progress.

Another step: To evaluate supervisors on whether they were doing this, by asking the operators if they were. Those results were posted in the supervisors' offices and discussed with them. This and other metrics created a Performance Leadership Profile assessment. This was one of the first multi-level rater surveys ever. Of interest, the Green Bay Packers football team heard of the work and experimented with it on their defensive team—measures, feedback, positive reinforcement.

"Dick was always interested in what we were trying, what the results were, and supportive of trying the next new idea or with the next new department. And he was involved. He's a manufacturing guy and would spend time on the floor with the employees," adds Marty.

"Dick was always interested in what we were trying, what the results were, and supportive of trying the next new idea or with the next new department. And he was involved. He's a manufacturing guy and would spend time on the floor with the employees," adds Marty.

After four years, Wikoff left KI for other assignments, but returned in 1995 as VP/HR and Quality. He performed that function for several years, which included making changes in the Gain- Sharing systems to align payouts more with what operators could control, and to make payouts closer to the accomplishment period. After that assignment, he began working with the sales departments to develop appropriate processes and metrics there. Eventually, KI became known as having the premiere sales training effort in the industry.

One effort that went haywire: They tried to computerize the sales pipeline process and metrics, like today's CRM programs, but it was too clunky to use given that era's computer capabilities and was dropped.

Also, on-site much of the time was Dick Chartier, an organizational behavior consultant from the Bay area, who would work with senior executives on their effectiveness. Chartier's time also got shared with several other Green Bay companies, including Schneider and Schreiber.

KI's Wellness Program

Dick was a very innovative, "before his time" thinker regarding corporate wellness efforts, driven partially by his own breathing deficiencies since childhood. To combat the trouble he had breathing and walking as a youngster, he became an avid exerciser, as a runner when young, and as a biker (and kayaker) as he grew older. Beth Seymour recalls, "Dick was at least a decade in advance of the marketplace in tying health insurance premium levels to health assessments and participation in fitness regimes. There were impacts well beyond the program. It kept me educated about what I should be doing and was a constant reminder of what I should and should not be doing. We also discovered significant diseases in people they didn't know they had, so appreciation for the in-plant nurse was high. We had a lot of runners, too. The majority were very grateful for all the elements of the program. It was definitely a part of the KI culture."

"Dick was a big believer in sharing information," says former CFO Mark Olsen. "Many leaders want to hoard data; Dick was just the opposite. If people don't know their operating data, how can you expect them to do their jobs at the highest level? You must trust them. Treat them like owners."

Even today in his 80's, Dick rides 15 miles a day in retirement.

Mark Olsen

Financial Transparency

"Dick was a big believer in sharing information," says former CFO Mark Olsen. "Many leaders want to hoard data; Dick was just the opposite. If people don't know their operating data, how can you expect them to do their jobs at the highest level? You must trust them. Treat them like owners.

"Several of us made presentations to employee groups each month, and we traveled to remote plants to do it as well as they were added," he recalls.

The Plant GainSharing payouts were monthly, so employees could see the impact. Daily and weekly metrics, where available, would tell them how the month was going. At month-end, 25% was held back in case the next month yielded a loss but was returned the following month. "If there was a negative at year-end, we just wrote it off, so employees weren't additionally penalized."

Government market leader Dan Schiltz says, "Dick was so far ahead of his peers in sharing information. 80 pages of financial were posted to the financial portal and prior to that shared with many via the monthly Heath meeting."

Beth Seymour, VP Manufacturing notes, "We had boards all around the plant that told everyone the metrics of how we were doing."

Management Techniques

• Weekly Recap reports on Friday by all managers on projects agreed to be working on—a bit about the past week, but just as importantly what will be worked on next week. Plus, if possible, a Hero of the week. Dick would write a note to each Hero. This transparency of so many people receiving the reports supported his objective of making sure people knew how their job fit into the total effort. People focused on the Marketing/Sales reports about what new business had been attained (and even on projects that were lost). They would take this information home, so the family was aware of how the business is doing.

• DDR's: Goals would also contain DDR's—the Date for completion as well as dates for check- ins, the Deliverable at the end, and the person Responsible.

- Weekly one-hour meeting with each direct report. Dick would come to the office on Sundays to review the Weekly Reports and be ready with questions.

- "He created focus. We established our list of priorities and made them paramount. If someone wanted something else on the agenda, it had to go last, to be only dealt with if there was any time left. The battle was to get your tactic onto the list. It really worked! We were a very focused, aligned group of managers, which accounted very much for why we were successful."

- "I remember once I was working on a $2 million proposal. I sent it to him, then met to go over it in person. He asked, 'How do I know you can make this work?' I turned to the second page, which had my signature on it as well as those of all my managers. He said, 'Go ahead!'"

- "At management meetings, he would drill into people to determine the depth of what they knew, that their understanding wasn't superficial. Sometimes it would end with, 'I don't agree with you!' It was far better to admit what you did and didn't know, and pledge to understand it by a specific date. Dick would remember that date."

- "Our memos often came back with a 1, 2 or 3 written on it. "1" meant, 'Yes, take care of it.' "2" meant, 'See me so I understand it better, and then go take care of it.' "3" meant, 'Don't do anything until you talk with me!'"

- Working with Dick: "I would meet with him weekly, and we would come up with 10-12 topics for me to work on. After I left his office, I would work ONLY on those 10-12 topics and get back to him. That responsiveness developed a lot of trust and rapport with him. Indeed, I didn't want to let him down because of that trust he put in me. It wasn't from fear; it was from pride in being part of the team, and I didn't want to disappoint. Others on the senior team felt the same way."

- "When you earned his trust, you were in trouble. He would rely on you even more and you would get more assignments, some unrelated to your current job, because he had faith in you."
- "He always asked good questions. Sometimes you would get frustrated because it would slow the decision-making time down, but you usually learned something that would change the decision slightly or a lot. His questions always stimulated thinking."

- "When we were making decisions that would impact a person's career, he always asked,'Is this right for the person as well as for KI?'"

- Vision: "He was very insisting, very communicative that we strive towards the very precise visions he set for us. To reach this year's goals. To reach the $1 Billion level, which we never did."

- Analytical/Systematic: "Have a clear action plan for achieving the Vision, for going from here to there. We heard it constantly: DDR, Dates of accomplishment, the Deliverables, Who's Responsible. He made sure we could program the cascade of what needed to be done down to the actual doer. The drive to make this occur was actually pretty rare in leaders."

- Accountability: "Once you convinced him, he made sure you got the resources you needed. He was frugal, but he would invest. You performed. Nothing ever fell through the cracks with Dick. No, not with Dick. He would remember and stop you in the hall and ask."

- "He wanted a lean structure, no more than five levels between the CEO and the technicians on the floor, which requires that information must be cascaded as low in the organization as it can. Otherwise, a lean structure can't work. That means that if a Customer Service rep gets a question, she can directly call the production scheduler on the floor to get the answer."

- "We had a Performance Standards Cascade: There were Key Metrics that the top brass required and then each Metric was owned by each direct report, who then created other metrics for their people to ensure performance—and they created additional metrics for their people to insure performance. This created alignment."

Finally, The 100% ESOP

For a long time, it weighed on both Dick and the KI Board as to how to make the transfer of ownership that would be necessary at some point. Says former CFO Mark Olsen, "We went through three complete iterations with P/E firms to create a selling and ownership transition agreement. Keeping the headquarters and plants in Green Bay was always part of the deal. He wanted management to still have an important stake in the company. We would talk often about Green Bay, and how when local companies like ours would leave, that it's a hit on the community, that locally- owned, locally controlled companies are critical, all down the line in size and influence. He would say, 'I want to give back to the community where we made the money.' Ultimately, we would get to the signing point, and he wouldn't do it. He backed away each time even though it would have converted his shares to even greater wealth, but it didn't feel right for the community or the company."

"We went through three complete iterations with P/E firms to create a selling and ownership transition agreement. Keeping the headquarters and plants in Green Bay was always part of the deal."

Then, in the 2017-time frame, the discussions turned to an ESOP and that eventually carried the day. In late April 2018, the company officially became 100% owned by an ESOP, run by Trustees, with debt held by banks, with the ownership group, including Dick, being paid out over five years. When the ESOP debt is paid down, employees ESOP accounts will begin gaining in value as the company prospers.

Dick is no longer the CEO. That position transitioned to Brian Krenke, a trusted 20+-year member of the KI Team, who came up through the sales ranks. He reports to the Trustees and oversees a management team that also has significant tenure, so the transition is relatively seamless.

On Giving Back

Like other leaders in this book, Sharon and Dick Resch are both active in supporting causes and institutions they care about. As indicated above, Dick told his senior staff many times that "I want to invest my money in the community that helped me make it." He was instrumental in creation of the Green Bay Community Foundation as a founding member. While many of their benefactions are evidenced by the Resch name, beginning with the primary funding of the Resch Family Trail along the East River because of his love of biking, and reaching a pinnacle with the Resch Center and KI Center, many more are not. Says one executive, "Those with their names on them are just the tip of the iceberg. Almost every day, checks are being written, large and small, to benefit challenges with which they are in sympathy."

Another recalls, "He is very human. I remember being in his office once when a mother and her 15-year-old daughter dropped by to say Thank You because Dick had paid for the renovation of a special violin for the daughter. He asked her to play, and she did, beautifully. During it, Dick had tears in his eyes. He was crying."

More on Dick

- He was a tremendous teacher and mentor. He clearly influenced my life, how I think and how I operate today."

- "He was a very compartmentalized thinker. You could have a conversation with him on several topics and when you visited with him three weeks later, he could pick up on its threads immediately."

- "He was actually very introverted, which many would interpret to being aloof and distant. I remember one time, instead of speaking to the sales organization as most CEOs would want to do, he asked if his talk could be videotaped. He didn't like being in front of a lot of people."

- "Cares intensely about getting things done and achieving goals."

- "Cares intensely about being healthy, and learning—continual learning. He would constantly buy people books to read, assign articles, and bring in speakers."

- Dedicated, committed: Worked six days a week, from 8 AM to 6 PM.

- Motivated to Win, at all costs: "This didn't make him the most popular person always, not always anyone's favorite person, but he always saw a bigger picture and required 120% effort before giving up."

- "He was a Risk-Taker, would make Bold Moves."

- "He was Disciplined to not let anything fall through the cracks, with a mind that rarely forgot what you were assigned to do, and what you were working on. He loved processes. We probably had more written procedures than we needed, but we had a great foundation."

- He was Data-Driven: "He liked to track everything, would even do it personally—how many miles he rode his bike every year (goal was 2100 miles). Whatever the result, the next goal was a level higher. Yes, he was hard to work for."

- "Often, he would walk through our department with his head down. He wasn't trying to avoid people; he was just intensively thinking."

- "Dick was very smart, thorough and articulate. That can be very intimidating, which obviously yields discussions that aren't as insightful as they needed to be. It was okay to disagree with Dick, or to move a conversation in other directions to make additional points. You didn't get penalized for that. What you get penalized for is not being fully transparent and committed."

- "It was okay to make mistakes. Dick was well aware that not everything or anybody worked perfectly. Just don't try bullshit. Admit what didn't work well or wasn't working, and pledge to work to make it work."

- Vision: "He was very insisting, very communicative that we strive towards the very precise visions he set for us to reach this year's goals."

- "Dick would analyze you as a manager and goal-deliverer, and push to your limit to get the best out of you for the good of the company. Some people handled it better than others. What you do is never enough. He is always pushing for continual improvement, but we know it's the same pressure he puts on himself."

- "He had a very, very astute mind. When we were analyzing a spreadsheet, in a nanosecond he could find the cell that make it wrong or skewed the information. He could definitely be intimidating with his intellect."

- "He was a savant in many ways."

- "With only a few exceptions, his decision criteria were data-based."

- "He was the one with the open mind to try things."

- "If there was the potential for improving performance, he would support the research, the trial and error."

- "He has a very astute mind. I remember early on, when he was still EVP, I rode with him to a meeting … in his Honda Accord. He started talking about the engine and its features, its overhead cam. He knew all the technical details. He clearly had the mind of an engineer."

- "Like many leaders, he was intrinsically motivated to accomplish."

- "There was never more than one thing on his desk at a time."

- Compassion: "When my wife contracted cancer, he came into my office and said 'We love you two. When you need anything, you have it.' He couldn't have been more helpful, sympathetic and supportive."

- "He was never good at small talk. If that's what was going on, he would disappear."

- "For all his impact, he didn't like being front-and-center; he was insecure in doing that."

- "He clearly had a soft side: If you, personally, or one of your employees had a significant personal challenge, he would be all-in to help out if we could."

- "He was very compassionate. When I resigned to spend more time with my very young children, I got a letter from him saying he couldn't compete with that reason, and that I would be welcomed back whenever it was right in my mind."

Don Schneider

We are grateful to the following for their insights from their experiences which created this chapter:

Wayne Baudhuin
Craig Dickman
Phil Enscoe
Mary Gronnert
George Grossardt
Don Jauquet
Wayne Lubner
Ed Thompson
Pat Schneider
Paul Schneider
Larry Sur

Green Bay's Golden Age:
Don Schneider
Schneider National

"Build a Sustainable Private Company, By Being the Biggest in Our Marketplace, By Being the Best"
~Don Schneider

The Short Version

Without the successful effort to extract itself from the Teamsters Union contracts and become a non-union trucker, fully ten years of turmoil in the 80s and for more than a decade after that, Schneider would not have survived.

It would *not* be here today, able to look back on a legacy of growth driven by innovation, a legacy that has made it and its CEO, Don Schneider, iconic in the modern history of U.S. trucking.

It was through these intensive years of struggle led by Don, his president, Ed Thompson, and a small group of others, in opposition to Teamster leadership and intransigence that was often to the detriment of its own members and oblivious to the reality that unionized truckload trucking could not survive in a deregulated environment, that this was enabled.

It's a great story. Industry officials said frequently, "How did you do that?" Of more than 200 union truckload carriers before Deregulation in 1980, less than a handful survived, and Schneider has stayed the biggest.

This and several other initiatives were able to propel its growth to *dominate* the truckload industry and *sustain* itself as a private company—two of Don Schneider's driving forces.

Another goal was critical, too: make sure drivers "were taken care of," so they would never want to have a union represent them. Indeed, in 1982, drivers supported the Schneider pay-reducing contract positions more than the union ones because they knew their job survival was at issue. At its height in 1986, Schneider Transport had 1,700 Teamster drivers; today, it has six in a force of 10,000 company drivers.

Key leaders during the 1980s: From left, Don Jauquet, Tom Vandenberg, Ed Thompson, Wayne Baudhuin, Wayne Lubner and Don Schneider. Not pictured: John Patterson.

By bringing a smart business acumen with typical Northeast Wisconsin work ethic, Schneider was the first in its industry to:

• Equip every truck with a satellite communications capability that facilitated much faster contact with drivers and let them know where every truck was.

• Develop sophisticated recruiting, career development and training programs, way beyond any competitor.

• Develop sophisticated operations performance reports and/operating software that could even be sold to client companies, and used to create other operating divisions, such as its Dedicated operation, which today provides $700 million in revenue.

• Take advantage of the 1982 AT&T disbanding to use its WATS line capabilities to start a new commercial business, Schneider Communications.

• Begin developing a logistics business, eventually as a stand-alone entity called Schneider Logistics, providing 3PL services to others, today providing $1.2 billion in revenue.

• Utilized technology breakthroughs to take over massive logistics organizations of large companies, most notably GM's huge Parts business, Kimberly Clark, Scott Paper and others.

• Grow its non-union truckload business to a nationwide enterprise with 13,000 employee and independent drivers, 9,000 trucks, 36,000 trailers, 22,000 containers, and more than $4 billion in revenue.

Today, it's now a public company, something Don did not want, with 15,000 employees nationwide.

In 2002, he turned the CEO reins over to Chris Lofgren, becoming Chairman where

Chris Lofgren

he served until his death in 2012. Lofgren had joined the company in 1994 as VP/Engineering, eventually became CIO, and served 17 years as CEO after succeeding Schneider.

The Early Years

Don Schneider was born to Al and Agnes Schneider in 1935—the midst of the Depression—in Fond du Lac. Soon Al and his new bride moved to Green Bay where Al sold his '32 Plymouth in order to buy a used truck with which to hire himself out. In 1938, he was working for a company that went bankrupt, so he used Agnes' dowry to purchase it. Schneider Transport was born.

He bought another small trucker in 1944, during WWII, and established his company at 817 McDonald St. He rapidly obtained business from local paper companies, attracting the interest of the Teamsters, who told him he would now be a unionized trucker. Over time, he kept purchasing additional used tractors and trailers, and adding drivers. It wasn't until 1960 that he actually purchased a new tractor.

All along, he and Agnes were adding other children: David in 1937, Paul in 1939, Jim in 1946, John in 1948, and Kathleen in 1951. The top floor of their tiny Stuart St. house became a dormitory.

As entrepreneurial families know, you grow up helping with the business, and the evening dinner table conversations would often center on the business. Don grew up understanding trucking. He and his brothers would spend weekends and summers cleaning the offices, washing trucks, being mechanic's helpers, and learning to drive.

The family was strongly Catholic, and the siblings all attended Cathedral grade school, then Central Catholic High School (later to become Premontre, then Notre Dame Academy).

Don became a Boy Scout and began enjoying camping; summer weeks at Bear Paw Scout Camp were a highlight,

A photo of entrepreneur Al Schneider's first trucks and depot in Green Bay.

and a respite from working at the trucking company. He was a saver and didn't spend his wages. He also developed what became life-long friendships with three others; they became inseparable and called themselves "The 4 T's"—nobody remembers why.

In his senior year, there was a party of these friends, also attended by a sophomore named Pat O'Brien, sister of one of the invitees. They took notice of each other, but not much.

After graduation, the "4 T's" decided to attend St. Norbert College, and all four continued to live at home; SNC was effectively a commuter college in the late 1950s. Don had access to an old Jeep and would drive them all to classes each day. Don also participated in the ROTC program, which required two weeks of military camp each summer. He majored in Accounting and Business. More importantly, he began dating—eventually creating a serious relationship with—Pat O'Brien, who after high school became an office worker at Charmin Paper Company.

They were married a few weeks after Don graduated from SNC in 1957, but he had a two-year military commitment. He was assigned to Korea for 13 months, including some time on hazardous duty which paid more. When he returned, he was stationed in Colorado and the family was reunited; Pat became pregnant with Mary, who would be born in 1958.

Don had no interest in joining the family business; he had wider sights and applied to the top tier of graduate business schools. He was accepted at famed Wharton, part of the University of Pennsylvania in Philadelphia. They moved there, to a small house. Their only money was what Don had saved from his high school years working at the trucking company and from the military. That had to get them through 18 months at Wharton, including tuition.

Pat recalls, "Those were very tough years, especially for me. Don left every morning for school at 7:30 AM and would stay working at the library until into the evenings. I was alone, eventually with three children. We went to mass on Sunday, and that was his main time at home." He did well, graduating in the Top-Ten in his class, and creating relationships with several of the professors. He graduated in 1961 and interviewed with several large companies recruiting at Wharton; he understood the national business scene.

Then he got a phone call from his father, now in his 50's and not in the best of health. "Don, the business isn't doing well. We're always struggling. I can't keep going like this. I need you here."

That settled it; he returned to what was always a very struggling operation, every pay period nip and tuck as to whether there was sufficient money. Don didn't get paid originally. Fortunately, professors at St. Norbert asked him to teach some accounting classes each morning before he went to work. That helped the family meet financial ends for a while.

(Wayne Baudhuin, one of many St. Norbert grads hired by Don, recalls "He was a good teacher. I took both his math-of-finance and statistics classes. They were at 8 AM on Tuesdays, Thursdays, and Saturdays. Saturdays? He said to us, 'Your grade will be composed one-third of the Saturday quizzes, one-third the midterm test, and one-third the final.' He made sure we got up early on Saturday mornings.")

'Your grade will be composed one-third of the Saturday quizzes, one-third the midterm test, and one-third the final.' He made sure we got up early on Saturday mornings.'

The company began feeling Don's impact almost immediately. Wayne Lubner recalls, "Al was mercurial, would rant and rave, and then later go mend the fences. Everyone knew and respected him. No matter what the situation, everyone got paid and layoffs were rare. Loyalty was high. Don, though, was a very systematic thinker, a visionary, and a great marketer—not warm and fuzzy. You could feel his intensity."

Don, 26 years old and a strategist, had ideas.

Fast Growth Through Acquisition

First, Don worked on the top line to ensure the current capacity became maximized. Then, he began working on expansion. In 1963, he purchased Packer City Transport, not large but with approved routes into 12 states. In 1968, he took over the Weyerhauser fleet in Marshfield, its first remote facility. In 1968 came Garrison Transport in Indiana with 60 drivers and equipment.

Also in 1968, he took on the company's first bulk/tanker hauler, Kampo Transit in Neenah, and Chicago, and renamed it Schneider Tank Lines.

By 1970, the company had 400 drivers and $13 million in sales.

Already, Don was bringing on a different breed of executive, ones with professional backgrounds and national purviews, using national recruiting firms, somewhat unheard of in the industry.

The impact of those new execs, including in a new selling division, was quick. Revenues increased to $23 million in the next year, 1971.

This was requiring major upgrades in accounting and control systems, forcing the company's first foray into computers, also very early in the industry. Part and parcel of that was improving communications between drivers and the company schedulers. He thought about how to put telephones in the cabs.

These mid-1970s also saw Schneider's first combat with the Teamsters.

Our story begins now, in the 1970s ...

Schneider actually **made its initial entry into Non-Union trucking in the early 1970's**, purchasing two refrigerated truckers in 1972 and 1974 and starting a bulk carrier in 1976, all three of which used independent operators—a precursor to what was to come, and giving the company experience in the ways of that less costly, more flexible type of operation.

In the mid-Seventies, there began to be talk of the government deregulating trucking, which would take ICC oversight out of the picture and pit union carriers directly with non-union ones.

Under ICC regulation, a trucker was given specific routes and competitors couldn't use those routes unless approved by the ICC, which rarely occurred. Effectively, the approved carriers had monopoly-like protection. That's why Don was purchasing other carriers, to get their routes. Then, because of the proliferation of non-union carriers in the south, the ICC began approving more and more routes, putting more non-union carriers in competition with union ones, and demonstrating the cost differences to customers.

Don Schneider was nothing if not a visionary (and he was much, much more) and saw this trend. He began analyzing what would happen under deregulation, and what his company must do to keep from being annihilated when deregulation occurred. Revenue was typically $1/mile for a truckload carrier. He determined that revenue would decline to a competitive $.75 per mile, and they had five years or less to get to that level. He told his senior team, "We have to take out five cents of cost every year."

Don Schneider was nothing if not a visionary (and he was much, much more)

The company already had a focus on safety, fuel costs and overhead. But the big barrier was the National Master Freight Agreement negotiated with the Teamsters which set driver compensation nationwide and required participation in the expensive Central States Health and Welfare and Pension Funds.

They needed a lower-cost driver pay system. Drivers would be impacted, but their jobs would be intact. (Ten years later, Schneider's 200 union competitors would be reduced to a handful who survived, with Schneider by then strongly union-free and the largest.)

"How Did You Do That?"

Schneider Transport operated under a negotiated rider to the national truckload contract that allowed it to pay drivers on a "Miles and Hours" basis as opposed to a "26% of revenue basis", which was in the rest of the National contract. At the 1976 renewal, the company attempted to negotiate a rider that would provide less than the LTL national scale mileage and hourly rates, but was unsuccessful. The company was given the ultimatum to accept the basic contract (26% of revenue) or be placed on strike. The drivers didn't want it, either. The drivers and their locals rebelled against the National, had a brief strike, and went to negotiations in Chicago, but lost to their union leaders. They also went on mini strikes again in 1978 and 1979.

(One story, by Wayne Baudhuin, who was managing the union division and had his office at the Broadway driver's terminal: During one wildcat strike when pickets lined the entrance to the Broadway facility, he got a phone call late one afternoon when he was coaching a girls softball game. "Wayne, we need you here to help us get out." "I drove right over, got a truck to lead it, went to every driver and asked, 'Are you OK with this?'. All were. Then, I was the first truck to drive through the picket line. We had 15 truck/trailers behind me all the way to the Illinois state line! I said, 'Okay, you can make it now!'")

Schneider Transport crossed the 1,000-driver level in 1976.

In 1979, the National Freight Agreement again required Schneider to pay on a 26% basis and the annual increase in the fallback Comparison calculation was set for each year (in the 3% range). As you know, the Cost of Living skyrocketed in the ensuing three years (13%, 12% and 9%), so driver's living standards took a hit based on the contract language. A corollary is that it kept Schneider's costs low so it could keep its pricing competitive; if it had to pay the increased rate, Schneider contends it could have gone out of business.

So, how was Schneider doing in lowering its cost of business to get down to that $.75 per mile level? Not well, and the 1980 Motor Carrier Act, which deregulated the industry, was approaching fast.

Examining Schneider's Working Philosophies

In 1977, Don Schneider hired Ed Thompson, a P&G lifer who had been site manager for the two huge P&G plants in Green Bay and had major experience dealing with unions. Like many, Ed didn't want to leave Green Bay, and Don provided him an opportunity. Don's rationale was that Ed was a very good businessperson, understood unions, had instilled within him P&G's sophisticated philosophies and practices, and was a mover-and-shaker. He had also been an adviser to Don over coffee and breakfast for several years.

Fellow executives say that hiring Ed Thompson brought true professional management to Schneider, something Don had sought since his Wharton days. And not too soon, as the perils and opportunities of Deregulation faced the organization and industry. He would be assisted immeasurably by Don Jauquet from the beginning, and then other operators like Wayne Lubner and Wayne Baudhuin, and attorneys John Patterson and Tom Vandenberg. Ed was responsible for overseeing the Teamster relationship reduction, as well as the gearing up with professional systems that allowed the fast growth in the late 1980's and beyond. (Ed left in the late 1980s and continued as a consultant. During his tenure, revenues increased from $94 million to $700 million, and the foundation was laid for the continuing growth.)

"We need to have close relationships with every driver. That's one of the most important tenets of good management."

One of the first things Ed said was, "We need to have close relationships with every driver. That's one of the most important tenets of good management." That was the reasoning behind Operation Handshake, where executives would be dispatched periodically to truck stops to visit with drivers, as well as other comparable practices, including recognition efforts.

Every list going forward of the non-union effort's goals included developing great relationships with drivers. Within the organization, it was a tenet for relationships with all employees.

These were the other tenets:

• Tell the Truth. Tell drivers how non-union competition is shrinking business. Explain to Teamster higher-ups the financials of the business, and the prognosis if Teamster costs, including the pension contributions, were to continue. Always tell it like it is. Unvarnished. Transparent. Never gloss over something. Be accessible. Recalls Wayne Baudhuin, who ran the union Transport division for many years, "Don and Ed would tell me, 'Tell the truth. You'll never get in trouble if you tell the truth. You can always explain it.'"

• Drivers who remain at Transport, even as business for the union division shrinks, will have a job at Schneider. (Today, there are six.)

• Explain to union drivers what was needed for them to be successful, so they could earn back some of the wages they would lose.

They had the economy working for them. The early 1980s was a well-publicized recession, and the drivers began to understand their livelihoods were being seriously threatened.

Betting The Company: The 1982 Negotiations

So, the Schneider negotiating crew decided the time had come to part ways with the Teamsters National contract and create a contract that would allow the company to survive, and eventually thrive—with union drivers de-emphasized. They proposed an "individual contract" that reduced driver pay by approximately $5,000 annually and created a new "Miles and *Stops*" pay system ... which not even drivers liked. They voted it down, 71% to 29%, despite showing drivers the company was at a 15-20 cents per mile disadvantage with non-union carriers.

Schneider wanted a second vote later in the year but was turned down. Now, they needed leverage at the top of the union, and Ed Thompson got it for them. The thrust was two-fold. First, explain again to the drivers what was happening. Ed recalls, "We would bring groups of drivers every Tuesday and Friday to Nino's restaurant near the stadium, and expose them to the financials, the economics of the business, the costs of fuel, the importance of when to shift gears, the costs of idling. We taught them about load ratios, and how to pick the most efficient routes. We told them why we put fuel monitors and speed limiters on the engines, and dials so they could see what the usage was." Again, *tell the truth*, as often as you can, to anyone who will listen.

Again, tell the truth, as often as you can, to anyone who will listen.

Drivers were also told that unions in truckload hauling were becoming a thing of the past, but that Schneider as a policy would continue to employ and protect them to the extent feasible. (Today, 40 years later, there are still a half dozen or so union drivers still employed as part of the unionized company, which has always been called Schneider *Transport*. The gigantic non-union operator is known as Schneider *National Carriers*.)

Managers from that era remember vividly their Lost Summer. Every weekend and many weeks, they were on the road to terminals to meet one-on-one with drivers to help them understand that they and the company would succeed more if they voted for the Schneider approach. Eventually, they came to understand that it wasn't an Us vs Them contract, but a contract that would better insure keeping current business and getting more business, and that the whole company, even the support employees, would be losers if the company wasn't successful.

The other thrust was to get a top Teamster official at Washington, DC headquarters to allow the second vote. Ed asked Tom Duffey, a business attorney/consultant with close Teamster ties to work the DC angle; he was successful at it, and the second vote was taken in the fall. The drivers approved it this time, 54% to 46%.

(The industry was shocked. Again, "How did you do that?" Before negotiations started, Brad Johnson, outside counsel, asked Don, "You know if this doesn't work that the Teamsters can strike and put you out of business? Are you sure you want to try this?" Schneider answered, "I might as well know now versus later whether I'll have a company or not." The Teamsters later that year struck and put out of business a large LTL carrier that tried to reach an individual agreement.

(Says Baudhuin, "You've got to understand that these drivers actually voted for a pay cut, and still wanted to continue working for the company. That's incredible! It was, of course, due to the circumstances, but also due to the trust that we were straight talkers and said you will have a job as long as you perform.")

This was just one of many "bumps in the road" on the way to surviving the union influence and thriving within the non-union marketplace. Many union officials at all levels, from the eleven locals to the Washington, DC leadership, were paranoidally protective of their contracts, and arrogant about their ability to control employers. They were often unsophisticated in negotiations at the top level, even belligerent, but Schneider's principals always were pressing towards their goals. Fortunately, a few local union leaders who understood the economics of the truckload industry wanted the drivers to retain their jobs and the Teamsters to retain them as members.

Don Jauquet, who was a critical part of the process for 30 years, emphasizes, "I repeated to them time and time again, union operations are viewed as 'High Cost, Inflexible, and Subject to Disruption,' and customers don't like that." Indeed, after one ten-day strike, Schneider's biggest customer told them strikes were unacceptable and they would look for an alternative carrier.

Schneider now was free from the National agreement, and had its own Teamsters contract with a better pay design, but was still not competitive with non-union carriers.

In the 1983-1984 timeframe, Schneider Transport, in part to appease the union but in a larger part to take on some Dedicated business, created a new unit, Special Services Division (SSD), which required union drivers, but with a Teamsters-approved contract *without* the Central States Health and Pension involvement. They would replace it with Schneider's own 401(k) and Health Insurance plans.

During negotiations, the union wanted to add a new provision that indicated the new SSD operation was fine, but *only* if the Classic division maintained Teamster employment at 1,500 drivers. This demand by the IBT was totally unacceptable and after a tense meeting at Teamster headquarters in Washington, DC, it was removed from the agreement.

In 1986-1987, Schneider realized that even the new SSD division wouldn't be competitive either, so it finally notified the union and the drivers of both divisions that they would be shrunk through attrition. So long as drivers stayed, they would be employed and protected.

The future emphasis would be using non-union drivers and independent contractors as part of Schneider National Carriers.

Don Schneider, Ed Thompson and others more than once traveled to Washington, DC to confront and negotiate with the top Teamsters officials, and that did not stop. They gained a reputation of forthrightness and high ethics within the industry, and believability by many Teamsters officials (but not all!).

The End of the Teamsters Saga ... in April 2004

Negotiating the decline of the unionized segments was an excruciating series of painful episodes overseen by Jauquet and Baudhuin. Both the Tank Lines and Transport divisions continued to have union employees as well as contributions to the Central States Health & Welfare and Pension programs, both of which became increasingly short-funded for their future liabilities.

Nevertheless, in April 2004, with a final payment of $2 million to cover future liabilities of former Schneider drivers, the company removed itself from both programs.

"Is There Any Color Other Than Orange?"

... declared Don Schneider. In the 1970's, each independent contractor company of Schneider's had different logos and trailer colors than the Hunter's Orange which Al Schneider had adopted. It created confusion in the loading yards. Customers were required to load specific trailers for specific geographic areas that the different contractors served, so customers had to be careful to load the correct colors of trailers. After deregulation, customers rebelled and pushed Schneider for one universal trailer to load to any destination. A universal color would be "easy to do business with besides being more distinctive for yard spotters to recognize, so both a marketing and operational advantage. The internal debate was whether to be "white" or Transport's "orange." We know which won.

Enter Schneider National Carriers, the New Union-Free Company, in 1986

In 1986, Schneider consolidated seven non-union carriers it had acquired into a new unit called Schneider National Carriers. This would be the foundation for the explosive growth.

But much had already been put in place. Don Schneider had assembled a group of high-powered executives who knew how to build a high growth business. Ed Thompson oversaw a core of Wayne Lubner and Wayne Baudhuin who were driving the operations side. Larry Sur also arrived in the 1970s to build the software systems which would inform growth. Sales managers were hired who could drive increases in customers in the new environment. A training division was created that could handle 100 new drivers a month. And Jim Liebig, an organizational development and ethics guru who would foster intensive recruiting, hiring, and training practices that also instilled the culture, was added.

Larry Sur

The result: Schneider National Carriers added eight terminals and 3,000 drivers across the Midwest in less than two years, and then added another 1000 on average every year for the next seven years, before growing more slowly to a peak of about 14,000.

Innovation

Growth was also driven by innovation, moving into other businesses with better margins. One was the Dedicated division, where drivers are assigned to a single customer, and that customer is managed as a separate business. "You had to prepare well when you approached these huge prospects, and had to have something unique to sell, especially reliability." Their first foray was with 3M, which asked Schneider to take over its private trailer fleet. That successful experience soon got them Kimberly Clark's 550-trailer fleet, and later huge portions of the Walmart business—and then the big keystone, GM's Parts business.

Another growth story was the Bulk Division. Says George Grossardt, who ran it for many years, "We grew it to where we had 4% of company revenue, but 10% of the operating income." It was initially led by Don's brother, Paul, then by Phil Enscoe, who arrived in 1973, and eventually by Grossardt. Enscoe was originally in HR under Liebig working on Bulk's HR challenges and volunteered to take on its leadership. "We

Phil Enscoe

weren't 'best' at anything. Finally, because Nalco was a client, we said, 'Let's specialize in Specialty Chemicals. Let's do all the things those companies don't want to do but need to like sophisticated tank requirements, MSDS forms and hazardous materials requirements, and the like. It worked." Enscoe's biggest challenge, though: "Don wanted to drive cost out of everything. That wasn't always the right thing for us."

An earlier cost reduction he recalls that did work: "Initially, we did driver training externally at driver schools, especially Fox Valley Tech. With his philosophy of doing as much in- house as you could, we created our own driver training school. That became especially important in the 80's when we were incurring the incredible year-to-year growth."

Managing Growth

Thompson says, "Maintaining growth is a major logistical, leadership and management challenge. To sustain high growth, we needed to keep adding new business, so we hired more than 60 salespeople. We needed drivers to deliver that business, so we created massive increases in drivers and their training, often through acquiring carriers in new areas we could then enter. We needed equipment for them to operate, so massive cash flow and debt to purchase the needed tractors and trailers. We needed the support organizations, so that side of the business had to increase quickly. Continually. The HR challenge to make all this happen was humongous."

With his philosophy of doing as much in-house as you could, we created our own driver training school. That became especially important in the 80's when we were incurring the incredible year-to-year growth.

Recruiting, Training and Metrics

Recalls Mary Gronnert, Don's assistant of several decades: "Don was very involved personally in recruiting. We worked with a Chicago organization that coordinated interviewing of military people leaving the service. They were very good supervisors. Don would go down there, interview prospects, and come back with 10-15 resumes. We also started recruiting at colleges. We would get resumes from colleges in advance, and Don would go to the campuses and do the interviews."

Of new recruits at the executive level, which often began with an assignment as a Driver Supervisor over 30-40 drivers and their schedulers, about a third each came from college, the military and internal promotions.

In 1980, Thompson and Schneider brought in Jim Liebig, a Harvard Business School/Yale Divinity School graduate who had worked in industrial human resource positions and had a very high ethics bent that appealed to them. He was a pioneer in innovative hiring and training practices, and in development of self-

George Grossardt

managing work teams. It was during this time that Liebig helped develop Schneider's Code of Ethics.

Grossardt recalls, "We invested in people, and managers were expected to grow them. To advance, you needed to be a "net exporter" of people, developing them to be competent for promotions, and then moving on to greater responsibility. Training became increasingly systematized and ingrained. It was critical so that we would have supervisors trained as managers as expansion occurred and managers were promoted."

To advance, you needed to be a "net exporter" of people, developing them to be competent for promotions, and then moving on to greater responsibility.

When Craig Dickman was hired in 1982 after a day filled with 7-8 interviews by various department heads, he recalls that his first week involved a review of the strengths and weaknesses he exhibited during his exhaustive interview experience. From that was created a Personal Development Plan, and assignment of a senior employee as his coach. Throughout one's career, he said, each leader was exposed to at least two targeted development programs each year to focus on strengthening capabilities. Covered would be topics like public speaking, interviewing techniques, and negotiating, with videos to critique and improve performance. "These were critical to the successful growth we were achieving. Schneider was way ahead of the industry in doing this development programming."

Craig Dickman

Thompson says, "We worked long and hard at developing leaders, not just 'trucker managers.' Lots of training. At one point, Jim Liebig was observing room after room of key people in classroom settings, and said, 'Ed, this looks like one giant Junior Achievement exercise.'"

For Thompson, he was educated at P&G that Metrics are key. "We had to build an organization with an emphasis on personal training and development, and an Internal Operating Organization driven by metrics.

The key ones: Costs/Mile, Total Revenue, Revenue/Customer, and a People Development metric. "From those, we would develop the cascade of metrics that would support them, by department."

Critical: Technology Sophistication

Growth wasn't all in moving goods via trucks, though.

When Larry Sur arrived at Schneider in 1977 at the age of 36 after 12 years at Whirlpool, he found the information system inadequate. Schneider had been one of the first truckers to embrace computerization in 1971, installing a state-of-the-art NCR package. "We had just signed a five-year contract with NCR, but both the hardware and software were by then inadequate. We switched to IBM, and with a young, enthusiastic team (a key person was Don Detampel), developed in just a year a new operating system, at a cost of $1 million, called SOURCE (Schneider Online Utilization Resources) that provided information on the movement of every tractor, trailer and driver in relation to each customer."

That allowed drivers to get critical information in real time.

A major source of long-time frustration for Don Schneider, unable to be solved until now, was the downtime drivers had on the road when they needed to call into their schedulers for guidance on next steps. They had to stop at a truck stop and place a long-distance phone call to just five switchboard operators in Green Bay. Often as much as 45 minutes lost time.

A major source of long-time frustration for Don Schneider, unable to be solved until now, was the downtime drivers had on the road when they needed to call into their schedulers for guidance on next steps.

Detampel and Sur purchased WATS lines and created NITRO, a computerized switching capability so drivers could reach their schedulers directly.

They had lots of WATS line capacity, and thanks to the dismantling of AT&T restrictions in 1982, thought, "Why not offer this excess capacity in the commercial market?" They created Schneider Communications, run by Detampel, which eventually had 19,000 commercial customers and was a dominant force early in the IT/communications revolution. They sold the business to Frontier Communications in 1996 for $127 million, a decision some thought was wrong because of the potential that was beginning to exist in integrating many forms of communication.

No other trucker was doing this.

Enter Satellite Communications

Out in San Diego in the mid-1980's, Irwin Jacobs was creating a new business, called Qualcomm, that would utilize new satellite communications technology for tracking purposes. He felt the trucking industry would be a great candidate. The biggest player? Schneider National. Jacobs came to Green Bay to meet with Schneider, Thompson, and Sur and after a several hour meeting, walked out with a large Schneider check to begin testing the system. Eventually, more than $26 million would be spent outfitting all 5,000 Schneider trucks so that drivers never had to stop to call the office; they would do it from the cab via computers. Critically, downtime and empty mileage were *significantly* reduced.

The gigantic Customer Service floor in the middle of Schneider's headquarters building today. The cubicles are organized by major customer and U.S. geographic areas, coordinating orders and drivers.

No other trucker was doing this. Schneider was the first major customer of Qualcomm, which would later be a long-term major player in the wireless communications industry.

Sur emphasizes: "If you wanted to be first in the truckload business nationwide, you had to be first in communications!"

In 1992, Wired magazine said, "Schneider is an Information company masquerading as a Trucking company." They weren't done.

(About this time, over in Iraq, the U.S. military was combatting the forces of Saddam Hussein, and having challenges in its own wireless communicating. Sur recalls being in meetings in Washington, DC, to explain how Schneider's use of Qualcomm systems worked, and might be applied in the military.)

Schneider Logistics

Over time, Sur's systems had gotten sophisticated enough to drive systemic and operating decisions, day-to-day, for a wider and wider group of sophisticated customers. In 1993, Sur convinced Schneider to let him try to create a Transportation Management division wherein they would manage the entire transportation segment of a large company's logistic network. They would simply add the capability of being like a broker, and getting customers efficiently routed with the lowest cost carrier available for each load. They started with 3M, their first Dedicated customer, and soon added PPG. Eventually, they obtained the biggest contract in the trucking business, moving the huge parts inventory of General Motors from suppliers to plants, dealers, and distributors, and saving them 10% of their massive, $435 million expenditure for that part of their freight business.

Today, the division is known as Schneider Logistics. It's a great business to be in, providing a revenue stream with virtually no investment. A trucker, of course, has to have a massive asset base of trucks, trailers, and maintenance facilities.

One of today's more modern tractors and trailers.

By the late 90's, Logistics was the fastest growing part of the business, and accounted for 15% of operating income. Today, Logistics provides more than $1 billion in revenues. The business was developed by Sur and Larry Chaplin, who had run the maintenance initiatives for Schneider for more than a decade before joining Logistics.

No other major trucker was doing this, but several would begin adding commercial logistics services later.

Chaplin and Sur left in 1999.

The Growth Data

When Schneider moved its headquarters from Ridge Road to the current, huge complex at Waube Lane and Packerland, it had about 900 Green Bay-based employees, but within a few years that soared to 1,500.

Growth, while always a challenge due to competition and economic vagaries, including an entree into China in 2005, was continual. It reached the $1 billion mark in 1992, $2 billion in 1995, and $3 billion in 2005. Today, it operates at a $4.4 billion level.

The CEO today, Mark Rourke, succeeded Chris Lofgren in 2019. He is a thirty year plus veteran, joining Schneider in 1987 as a Driver Manager, and working his way through the ranks.

On Ownership

Don Schneider received publicity near the end of his career about being a billionaire, which he denied. Whatever the value of the business or his family's holdings, he had an interesting plan to ensure the continuity of the business.

In 1986, he began creation of a governing Board that would eventually have eight members; five had to be outsiders, one the company president, and no more than two Schneiders, with each person having one vote. He selected outsiders in whom he had faith would make decisions in the best interests of the continuity of the company and the financial health of the family. Included was a Compensation Committee which would determine his own compensation.

Tenure could be no more than 12 years so there would be a mix of new minds, and pay would be dependent on attendance.

After that, whereas he had only one vote regarding company issues, he and his family were the majority shareholders. He had a plan to purchase the remaining shares held by his brothers, allocating stock to a few management executives as well.

From 1991 to 1995, he proactively gifted the majority of his shares to three trusts, paying tens of millions in taxes which otherwise wouldn't have been owed until his death. While family were still the beneficiaries, the voting was held by the independent directors. By 1995, he controlled no votes as a shareholder, and only the one vote as a board member.

Of course, in 2019, well after his death in 2012, the company directors voted to take the company public, issuing shares to the public and also providing an independent value to the family's beneficially held shares.

Today, there are two classes of shares. The Schneider family controls 94% of the Class A shares, but the voting control of them for practical, day-to-day purposes lies with the majority independent directors on the Board. The Class B shares are listed and publicly traded.

Don Schneider's Passion

What was Don Schneider driven by? Sur explaines: "His passion was to develop Schneider as a Sustainable, Privately-Owned Company, by Being the Biggest in its Marketplace, by Being the Best. You did this by driving to be the most Cost-Efficient, and by being Nationwide so that when a customer called, you could be there instantly with what they needed. A major theme for him was that the nation's citizens could be better off if the logistics piece of the economic pie were reduced." Indeed, national logistics costs dropped as a % of GDP to 10% from 17% over that time.

On The Schneider Foundation

As with many large organizations, the Schneider company's contributions to community non-profits are coordinated through its foundation. Each year, when doing budgeting, the company allocates funds to the Foundation, most recently in the range of $1.5 million. A team of nine Schneider associates determines the allocations of that money. The Mission of the Foundation states that grants will be made to organizations serving in these areas: Arts & Culture, Children, Education, and Health & Human Services.

In the early years, the company's contribution was made to the local Community Chest, eventually renamed United Way.

Today, other fundraising projects by employees are also coordinated through the Foundation, such as the Dollars for Doers program, where if an employee volunteers at least 50 hours for a non-profit, the Foundation will cut a check for $500 for that charity.

In addition, members of the Schneider family who have benefitted from stock ownership make their own disbursements to organizations and causes they feel are appropriate. Recent ones include the Donald Schneider football stadium at St. Norbert College and the Donald J. Schneider School of Business & Economics there. Don is a 1957 graduate.

Administrating the giving efforts and overseeing the Foundation since its inception in 2004 has been Mary Gronnert, who joined Schneider in 1973 and retired a few years ago. Today, it is coordinated by LuEllen Oskey.

More About Don

• He was a person of Purpose, Principle and Compassion. One year, the overall Schneider results did not achieve the level of bonus payouts. Don called a meeting of his 30 top people and said, "You've put me in a very difficult position. Our results did not achieve the levels for the bonus payouts, but that's not the fault of the employees below you. They did their jobs and did them well. The mediocre performance this year is due to you. So, what I'm going to do is still give bonuses to the rest of the organization, but there will be no bonus for the people in this room."

• Mary Gronnert recalls, "He was very intuitive and had a great grasp of what numbers were saying. He could tell what was going to happen in the industry well in advance. He would think about that a long time before acting but then would commit and put in place the strategy to deal with it. The biggest example, obviously, was the change to being Non-Union."

• "He was an early advocate of holding employees accountable for their health habits and tying them to their insurance premiums. In a transportation industry publication, he was quoted as saying that if an employee smoked, that his insurance premium share would be increased. RJR, a tobacco company that was a very major customer, was riled at that statement. Don didn't back down. He stuck to his belief. And RJR pulled their business from us."

• Wayne Baudhuin, when he was new to the company and coordinating Dispatching, recalls, "One Friday at 2 PM, I was doing my dispatch job, when Don walked in quietly and began watching me. I didn't know he was there. Eventually, I noticed him and asked if I could help with anything. 'No,' said Don, 'I just wanted to make sure you're proving me right in hiring you, and you are.' 'Can you tell me what you mean?' I asked. 'No, I'll tell you later.' He never did."

- "Don had this way. He wanted you to do the talking. He'd be quiet until you did. Then, he would lean towards you with those piercing eyes and listen to every word."

- "Standards? Unusually high and strict."

- "He wanted to build a company that attracted the best people. He would train them in trucking."

- "He was never a micro-manager. He hired good people and delegated to them. He expected us to do our jobs."

- "He was very respectful of other people—drivers, mechanics, office workers—which is why people were so loyal to him."

- "He was very accessible. Drivers revered him because he was a straight-talker, and often met personally with them in small groups." Says another, "He wanted drivers to be 'Understood, Appreciated, and Recognized.'"

- "He was both People and Data driven and Tough!" Adds another: "When things weren't to his satisfaction, he could act like a tyrant. He could be very intimidating."

- "You couldn't say No to him. Not allowed. 'We need more drivers! Figure out how!'"

- "Don wasn't necessarily a great people person, at ease with people, but he hired great people who were."

- "We were a 'People Organization.' Yes, strategic initiatives, but we all made sure we never lost sight of having an active relationship with the drivers. We wanted communication up and down all the time."

• "He was driven to grow the business and maximize opportunities. Witness the financing of incredibly fast growth (for which he prepared with great technology and people development systems) and embracing offshoots like Communications and Logistics."

• His office was spare. He worked from a shelf in his office (picking up on Ed Thompson's habit), so meetings were stand-up, usually brief. If needed, there was a small table with two uncomfortable chairs beside it.

• "He was definitely a learner. Even when he would go skiing or hunting, he would take lessons and guides, to understand how to be as perfect as he could." He also won the Bellin 5K run in his age class.

• "He was a voracious reader, who wrote on and pasted Post-It notes on many pages. If he really liked a book, he would buy 50 copies and distribute them. He even took a speed-reading course." His favorite books: Collins and Porras' *Built to Last*, and Dan Goleman's *Emotional Intelligence*.

• "He was chronically late. Once, he was late to an airplane. He drove his rental car to the airport, left his car in front, and ran into the terminal."

• Like many leaders, his hard side would be complimented by a soft side. "He and Pat went on a couples' workshop on self-discovery, which he appreciated. He gave me a book on self-discovery and paid for my wife and me to attend it, too."

Bob Bush

We are grateful to the following for their insights and experiences which created this chapter:

Nancy Armbrust
Tracy Arndt
Carol Bush
Terry Bush
Tom Badciong
George Cawman
Ron Dunford
Larry Ferguson
Mike Haddad
Brian Liddy
Jack Meng
Jeff Ottum
Mark Peterson

Green Bay's Golden Age:
Bob Bush
Schreiber Foods

"Someday, We'll Be Recognized as A Yogurt Company That Also Sells Cheese!"
~Larry Ferguson, CEO (1999-2007)

The Short Version

In 1968, Bob Bush welcomed Jack Meng as a new employee, telling him about his pride in the growth of the processed cheese manufacturer from 1946 until now to $43 million solely on handshake agreements with suppliers and customers.

Today, in 2021, the company has more than $6 billion in revenues and almost 9,000 employees, operating worldwide!

You can go virtually anywhere in the world and eat a McDonald's cheeseburger, the cheese came from Schreiber as it has since the 1960s. Ditto with Burger King, Taco Bell, Subway, and a slew of others.

Go into a Walmart Superstore—Schreiber is its largest supplier of many of the branded cheese Walmart sells. Because Schreiber is essentially a private label manufacturer, you may be eating many other companies' branded cheeses, made to their formula by Schreiber.

And, added since 2000, Cream Cheese and Yogurt. Today, Schreiber is the WORLD'S SECOND LARGEST yogurt maker, behind Dannon and tied with YoPlait.

It has plants in many of the countries in which its customers sell, and ships to nearby countries as well.

That's how you build to $6 billion!

From tiny little Green Bay, a private company, owned 100% by its employees due to an ESOP created in 1999 and committed to a Green Bay headquarters for its worldwide marketplace.

Bob joined the company in 1950 from college and didn't succeed to the top job until 1978, remaining in it until 1985, growing the company to about $700 million. More importantly, he

118

built on his predecessors' ethics, values, and operating principles, as well as adding many of his own in modeling what great leadership could look like. That model formed a foundation on which successive CEOs (Jack Meng, Larry Ferguson, David Pozniak, Mike Haddad, and now Ron Dunford) and their organizations built a much more expansive company that succeeds on the reputation of still serving well many of its earliest customers.

How was this made to happen? Several major key developments:

• First of all, a cultural commitment to constantly lowering costs, often while providing a better product. (50s, 60s, 70s)

• Shortening the order-to-delivery (turnaround) time to best in the industry, developing more sophisticated logistics programs to drive production scheduling to minimize inventory, creating the powerful differentiator of higher Return on Investment. Driven by the creation of many distribution centers closer to the customers' delivery locations. Also, an emphasis on quality that proved quality can create more consistent costs and therefore lower costs. (80s)

• Moving to a customer-driven pricing focus (work from the customer's need back to the logistical requirements) from the lowest cost one, driving margins higher while still yielding industry-lowest pricing when Total Return is calculated. (80s, 90s)

• Following major customers' global expansion efforts with plants and distribution capabilities in more and more countries. (2000s, 2010s)

Like several others of our "Golden Age" companies, the foundation for later success was created by truly entrepreneurial, risk-taking, aggressive people taking best advantage of what was available, and possible. In 1946, Merlin Bush and Dave Nusbaum took on L.D. "Barney" Schreiber's offer to run the bulk cheese manufacturing plant he just purchased in Green Bay, Wisconsin. They went after the big guys in the nation—Kroger and Safeway—to provide their dairy section cheeses from little Green Bay. In the 50s and 60s, the concept of fast food began to take hold and upstarts like McDonald's needed suppliers of cheese for cheeseburgers. By 1974, McDonald's was L.D. Schreiber's top customer.

During the 1950s, young Bob Bush, who joined the company out of the UW—Madison's dairy college along with his brother, Dick, who would go on to head the sales operations, was constantly looking at cheese-processing and packaging problems, seeing them as opportunities, and redesigning, or designing, new machines to provide an improved product that customers would pay more for. Green Bay Machine would become a new business for Schreiber, selling cheese-making equipment throughout the world beginning in 1967. Bob was a tinkerer, an engineering mind always looking for a better way with eventually 17 patents in his name.

A famous example. Bob is incorrectly given credit for inventing the machine that slices cheese. He didn't. He noticed that in the fast-food market, cooks had to fumble with the sliced cheese loafs to get each slice. He conceived of a machine that sliced the cheese, and then offset it by a smidgeon. providing a handle for the cook to grab quickly. Later, he invented the machine for individually wrapping slices of cheese! Individually wrapped pieces allow the meal-preparer to use a slice at a time much more easily. Later on, we'll tell stories about how he vetted a new Australian cheese-making process that would drop cheddar cheese production costs by 40%. (Not all the improvements were his invention.) A culture of creating cost efficiencies was one of his legacies. Others have provided patent-rewarded improvements as well.

Schreiber was known for the fastest turnaround times in the industry. Two weeks from order to delivery. "But two weeks! That's not that good," remembered one executive. That was abetted as Schreiber purchased other small manufacturers around the nation and added distribution centers with inventory. They could then deliver faster because they were closer to the customer's locations. What drove a massive improvement was the Walmart business, which required a three-day turnaround. This required more aggressive logistics software driving estimates

What drove a massive improvement was the Walmart business, which required a three-day turnaround.

of safety stocks by location, balancing production scheduling of thousands of SKUs for customers, and storage requirements in each distribution center. Not always as efficient as possible, but workable, and clearly by far the best in the industry.

The result, as analysts know, is a Return on Investment calculation for the customer with reduced inventory carrying costs (storage and interest). A major argument and differentiator for Schreiber with all their customers! This won them much additional business.

A commitment to an unrelenting approach to quality began with Mer Bush's famous mantra, "16 Ounces To A Pound!" If the package indicated a volume commitment, and someone measured the actual amount, there would never be a shortage. It's everywhere in Schreiber's environment. Also, when the Lean movement began in the early 1980s, Schreiber was one of the earliest to jump on it, building consistency into their processes, and reliability of outcomes for their customers. That reliability paid off as another differentiator when promoting its services to prospective new customers.

Gradually, that commitment to reliability and cost-effectiveness resulting in low prices won more and more customers, who became larger as consolidation occurred, and as they expanded to other countries. "When everyone knows you're the sole supplier to Walmart and McDonald's, it gets attention! Often, we were the only private labeler at industry trade shows, enabling us to meet even more customers," said an executive.

Characteristically, if a company could maintain reliability at close to a 100% level, and competitors couldn't, it attracts new customers at an accelerating rate (especially as weaker competitors drop from the market). That's what happened, and Schreiber's growth escalated.

Whereas it grew from 1968's $43 million, as it developed its reliability base during the '70s and '80s, it didn't reach $1 billion until 1993. And then it took off! Seven years later it was at $2 billion. With the addition of Cream Cheese and Yogurt when Mike Haddad took over as CEO in 2009, they were at $4 billion, and in 2019 when he left, they were at $5.5 billion, primarily via international expansion. Today they're over $6 billion.

Mike Haddad's mantra in 2009 was "Modernize and

Globalize." During his oversight, capital expenditures set Schreiber records and added to already operated plants in India, Mexico, and Germany. To follow customer expansions, they moved into Portugal, Spain, Austria, France, Belgium, the Czech Republic, and Bulgaria. From those plants, they exported to other countries as well.

Mike Haddad

Through all of this was the influence of Jack Meng, who joined in 1968, became president in 1985, and oversaw the commitment to a more customer-centric approach as well as the sophistication of the business operations and the philosophical commitment to a 100% ESOP in 1999. He is also given credit for "institutionalizing" much of the commitments that reflect the integrity of the company.

Some of the mantras attributed to him:

- "Respect The Past, But Don't Protect It!"

- "Make Today Better Than Yesterday, and Tomorrow Better Than Today."

- "TQC-Squared: Total Quality Commitment By A Thinking Quality Culture"

- "WDW: What Drives Work?"

About Bob Bush

Bob Bush was born in 1926 near Buffalo, NY, to the practical, visionary, mischievous, compassionate son of a cheesemaker, Merlin Bush (known as Mer), and his wife, Ruth. Two years later, they added a son, Dick, and two years after that, a daughter, Ginny.

Mer had graduated from Cornell in dairy science where he studied under Professor Walter Price, who had developed a formula for processed cheese. After graduation, A&P, the huge grocery store chain, hired him into its local factory where they were producing Price's formula. A year later, however, Kraft sued them for patent infringement, even though, the formula was different. The factory folded. Mer and his family moved to Minneapolis in 1929, and then later moved to Chicago to be a buyer for A&P. After a successful ten years there, he was approached to run a small cheese factory up in Green Bay, Wisconsin, getting him back into manufacturing. A highlight was getting the largest government contract for cheese ever.

In 1945, another Chicagoan, L.D. "Barney" Schreiber, asked him to start another cheese company in Green Bay.

While in Chicago, Bob as a young boy was both industrious and experimenting. He made money by delivering magazines on his bicycle; he also tried selling eggs from his bicycle, but that didn't work (too much breakage!). His earnings went to buying airplane model kits and additional pieces for his Erector set. When Bob was 14, his dad purchased lots on Green Bay out near Dyckesville and built a small home on one of them. That got Bob interested in boats—and speed. He got ahold of a 14' skiff and put a 21-horse Johnson on it. But he wanted it to go faster. So, he raised the gas tank out of the water to lower friction, added a pump to the fuel system to increase the gas pressure to make it burn hotter, and took the muffler off which created some additional advantages. It also made the boat very loud. Besides unsettling the neighbors, he would pilot it in races on the Fox River. The boat was named PDQ 1, the first of 23 boats he would own, all of them with the beginning initials PDQ, for "Pretty Damn Quick!"

He also developed an interest in shooting, practicing at a shooting range on the top floor of the downtown YMCA building.

As he needed more money, besides setting pins at the Dyckesville Bowl, his dad let him do cleaning at the cheese plant, his first introduction to cheese equipment. He soon found that he was helping the employees solve their problems. At one point, he designed a cam change in a machine that increased its productivity by one-third.

In town, Mer and Ruth lived at 912 S. Jackson St., a nice-sized brick house for a young couple; they would later move to DuCharme Lane in Allouez. Bob went to Washington Junior High, and then to East High School. There, he had a girlfriend, played guard on the football team, and generally didn't apply himself to studies but still got respectable grades. The senior prom was his last date with his girlfriend. He was beginning to notice another girl.

From high school, he headed to the service; there was still a war going on in 1944. He signed up with the Army Air Corps, determined to become a pilot. Unfortunately, they found out he had a pilot's license already, for boating, and assigned him to Boca Raton, Florida, to a "crash boat unit" on standby to rescue boats in trouble. He had little to do.

Postwar, he came back to Wisconsin and entered the University of Wisconsin's Dairy Science and Mechanical Engineering programs, where he excelled. Some of his achievements:

• As part of an assignment, he created a very, very, rich ice cream formula which is still sold at the dairy store there today.

• One snowy day, he called a radio station, said he represented University adminis-tration, and told them that the UW classes were called off for the morning. The station ran that announcement immediately, other stations picked it up and repeated it, thus, UW students got the morning classes off. (Many years later, he received an honorary doctorate from the university. He didn't tell university officials until after he had been given the award that he was the culprit who had shut the school down.)

One snowy day, he called a radio station, said he represented University administration, and told them that the UW classes were called off for the morning. The station ran that announcement immediately, other stations picked it up and repeated it, thus, UW students got the morning classes off.

• One night, he and his friends stole the keys of the famous "Army Duck" at the university, drove it back to a sorority house, and parked it in front. Later that night, some other kids rolled the Duck down to and onto frozen Lake Mendota, where it began to crack the ice and sink into the depths.

• Another time, he took a special chemical that when spread on a hard surface, dried, and when pressed on it would create a "popping" sound. He snuck into a sorority house and painted it on the floor of the laundry room.

• There was animosity between Law students and Engineering students. So, one time Bob took a special, very foul-smelling cheese, went into the Law dorm, and put the cheese behind the radiator where it would warm up. The building had to be evacuated.

(Of interest, Professor Walter Price of Cornell was at UW—Madison, due to its dairy science reputation, by the time Bob entered, so he took classes from the same teacher his father had. Later, his daughter Tracy attended and took classes from him, too. Three generations!)

During the UW days, he also became smitten with Carol Bickford, who was two years behind him at East High. She ended up going to Beloit College, not far away from Madison and after graduation, began teaching English and coaching field hockey at Wayland Academy in Beaver Dam, also not far from Madison.

Bob graduated from UW in 1950 with two objectives, he said: "To begin a job at Schreiber, and to marry Carol Bickford 'because she is spunky.'"

Bob and Carol bought a house at 512 S. Jackson St. and began to raise a family there. Tracy was born in 1951, Terry in 1954, Tom in 1956, and Toni in 1963. In 1954, they moved to a larger home on Greene Ave. in Allouez (and in 1969 moved to their long-time home on Bay View).

Early Days Set Standards

Like all of our Golden Age companies, the early entrepreneurs—usually the founders and their immediate successors—set the stage for continued impact and growth. Barney Schreiber's first hire to start a new processed cheese company in Green Bay in 1945, was Mer Bush, who immediately hired Dave Nusbaum as production manager. (Kraft's patent for processed cheese had expired in 1938.) Their first major customer was the U.S.

government, which wanted the cheese packaged in seven-pound cans—the company had no canning machine. It developed one and grew the business. Then, another Green Bay cheese company fell out of bed with Safeway, the big grocery store chain, and Mer went after that volume, which got them into the private label business!

During these early years, Bob Bush and his younger brother, Dick, worked summers at the plant. Even as a student, Bob made an impact. In 1948, he watched a box-filling machine operate, and then redesigned a cam that sped the machine by more than 30%. Bob's insightful and creative engineering mind was the sparkplug for myriads of both speed and quality improvement initiatives over the next two decades. Both were important because high quality results in reliable products, and higher speed results in cost, and price, improvements compared to competitors. In all, Bob earned 11 patents during his active time there. Plus a few more later on and for solving supplier problems, totaling 17 in all. Indeed, many of his machinery improvements resulted in machines that could be sold to others; the company created Green Bay Machinery to market those, most of them overseas.

Another critical early-day initiative was Mer Bush's commitment called "16 Ounces To The Pound." In the late 1940s, he noticed that competitors wouldn't always deliver full blocks of cheese to the government or competitors. He vowed that would not be the case at L.D. Schreiber. That commitment to quality has become a slogan at Schreiber.

The commitment to private labels also set a pattern to this day.

The 1960's and 1970's

The Sixties set other important patterns, especially broadening its reach into other areas of cheese use, more and more private labeling for smaller grocery store chains, and later in the decade, into fast food. That area had lots of competitors, notably Kraft, Borden, and Pauly. But Schreiber got tested in McDonald's.

Another critical early-day initiative was Mer Bush's commitment called "16 Ounces To The Pound."

Because of reliability and fast turnarounds, L.D. Schreiber made inroads into others as well. By 1974, McDonald's was the company's largest customer. Schreiber wasn't the only cheese supplier to McDonald's at that point, though by 1990 McDonald's declared Schreiber its World Standard. Eventually, fast food chains became half of the company's revenue stream. (Fast food chains don't like that moniker, so it's changed to Quick Service.) Today, interestingly enough, Schreiber's biggest customer is Walmart.

At the same time, the company began to increase its geographical footprint to be closer to customers. It bought and/ or built new plants in Missouri and Utah, setting the table for

Jack Meng

much faster expansion later. Indeed, its international expansion in the 2000s would be to follow its customers to other countries.

It was in 1968, as mentioned earlier, that Bob Bush welcomed future CEO Jack Meng to the company and extolled the company's progress in expanding to $43 million.

Also key, was cementing in place the crucial managers who would build the company over the next few decades alongside Bob and his brother, who would oversee the sales efforts: Bob Deutsch, George Cornell, Vince Zehren (the food chemistry whiz), Tom Badciong, Jack Meng, and others.

There also was an important ownership change. In 1962, Barney Schreiber, the 100% owner, agreed to sell some shares to 13 current executives for $1 million on his personal loan. Then, when they paid that off, he sold them more shares up to 49% ownership. "We asked if he would then sell us more, and he said he would, so we borrowed more money and bought the rest," said Bob. Jake Rose of Kellogg Bank in Green Bay became the catalyst who had confidence in the company and bankrolled the thirteen executives with loans to buy the rest of the stock. Later, as other executives were offered ownership, Kellogg (eventually called Associated) would be the loan source.

A story: Jack Meng, not long out of college, volunteered to go to Logan, Utah, to manage the newly purchased swiss cheese facility, which was losing money. "I didn't know anything about cheese-making, but I appealed to Vince Zehren and he educated me. We discovered that the facility was producing poor, Grade D cheese because the 'starter' wasn't sufficiently active to create

Grade A, which we could sell at premium prices." To support that that change, Jack used his MBA-learning and instituted consistency/variability metrics which assured reliability at a Grade A level.

The 1980's: The Foundation for Faster Growth

As the Eighties began, Schreiber Foods (which had now changed its name from L.D. Schreiber Cheese Co.) was becoming a force in the marketplace but it wasn't nearly the behemoth it is today. It didn't get to $1 billion until 1993. But the Eighties yielded a number of sophisticated changes that strengthened the foundation for that growth.

Embracing The Total Quality Movement

Schreiber was early in embracing this movement, in the early 1980s. They learned about and began implementing the Philip Crosby "Quality Is Free" approach.

Says Meng: "Many companies fail or sub-optimize its application by not indoctrinating the people on the operating floor; their commitment is short-term and top-level. We didn't. We learned it and drilled it down to the operating floor, so its mantras and metrics became second nature. It eventually permeated how we acted towards everything and everybody. Partners, customers, suppliers, everyone. It helped move Integrity even more to the forefront in how we operated. I remember that we fired one manager who proposed a tactic that would yield several million dollars for us but would be unethical."

Meng believed so much in the approach and wanted it to be embedded at a tribal level, that he coined a phrase, "Total

Quality Commitment-Squared", which referred to "Total Quality Commitment from a Thinking Quality Culture."

"We institutionalized it. We even changed our logo to include TCQ2 on it," recalled operations expert Tom Badciong. "When Bob Bush visited a plant, he always started with examining the cleanliness in the restrooms. Cleanliness and orderliness have to be in place every place. The rest of us began doing that, too."

Jeff Ottum

Recalls Jeff Ottum, then Green Bay plant manager: "Once when going down a narrow but very clean staircase at the plant, Bob held onto the handrail. At the bottom, he pointed out that there was dust on the underside of the railing. He was right. If you're going to be completely clean, be completely clean."

When new equipment was designed, or new vats were ordered, if food was involved then all the edges had to be rounded so they could be cleaned completely. Where there are corners or straight edges, there will always be residue.

Per Mike Haddad, CEO from 2009 - 2019: "Bob Bush, Tom Badciong and Jack Meng were maniacal on food safety and food quality. There was zero tolerance for people hurting themselves in the plants. And product quality had to be perfect because you can't let any customer ever get sick from our food."

Another Bob Bush example: When new equipment was designed, or new vats were ordered, if food was involved then all the edges had to be rounded so they could be cleaned completely. Where there are corners or straight edges, there will always be residue.

Transitioning to Customer Focus

Traditionally, as a manufacturer of a customer's branded item, competing against other private labelers, you have to be lower cost. The emphasis is on how to re-engineer processes to be more efficient. Then, recalls Meng, "Kraft began taking its excess production and selling it to our customers at a lower cost than ours. We began losing money. We had to do something. We needed marketing guys, not cheese guys."

Enter several with marketing backgrounds, including George Cawman, a marketing activist who had been in charge of new business development for Armour-Dial and had extensive experience as product manager for several of their consumer products.

"They began teaching us how to look at a customer's needs and work backward as successful companies would do. Eventually, this turnaround resulted in us pushing out ConAgra and Kraft from the market and laid the foundation for our differentiation and success going forward," said Meng.

A number of separate thrusts combined to make this work.

Differentiating The Market, And Pricing

When Cawman joined in 1982, Schreiber had five distribution channels:

1. "Quick Service" Chains, like McDonald's, Wendy's, Hardee's, Burger King, and Subway. (At one point, they had eight of the Top Ten.)

2. Retail, i.e., grocery chains, eventually including Walmart.

3. Food Service Distributors, like Sysco and Reinhart, who distributed to restaurants and smaller groceries.

4. Industrial, as a raw ingredient for pizza, mac 'n cheese, and the like.

5. Green Bay Machinery, supplying cheese-making equipment.

Says Cawmen: "I remember a Saturday morning meeting on my deck at home attended by ten key people, where I outlined our new approach. We would de-couple our pricing from the weekly cheese markets, and instead, begin pricing on value. We would depend on our cost-efficiencies to provide us a price, keeping it advantageous to our customers in concert with our other

George Cawman

differentiators. Its focus would be on reliability and consistent quality, at greater margins!"

This was no small challenge. Jeff Ottum, at the time the Retail market manager but later VP/ Human Resources, explained:

"In the grocery stores, we were in two areas. The Dairy area carried the store's branded cheeses such as shredded cheese and various popular types. The Deli area carried a myriad of specialty cheeses, many of them also manufactured to formula by Schreiber. Major grocery chains wanted their own sizes and cuts of each and wanted them labeled with their own logo. This calls for a massive number of SKUs, and because of the small volume of each it wasn't cost-effective to pre-manufacture and warehouse them all. We would

order in the different types of cheeses, plus our own, in large bulk loaves, and then make them to order at a plant nearest the delivery sites as much as possible.

"It was a job shop, pulling each cheese from its storage, cutting it as ordered, printing the private label with the grocery's logo, and applying it to each retail package. Then, combining all parts of the order and shipping it, either to the grocery chain's own distribution center or to individual stores. Expensive."

And not great margin, either. There were competitors for this business: Borden, Land O'Lakes, even Safeway, and Kroger had its own processing plants.

Cawman noted: "Because of our software analytics by product, we could analyze each of the SKU's we provided as to profitability and where we were losing money we could make adjustments that created profitability.

"We also changed our salespeople commissions from selling pounds to selling margin.

"We saw dramatic improvement within several months in our overall profitability."

(Indeed, within several years, the Retail business accounted for the greatest bulk of profit dollars for the company.)

Cawman went on: "As we grew, we began to invest more in what we were accomplishing. We were beginning to dominate our marketplaces. We purchased Clearfield Cheese, which gave us a major force on the East Coast. We bought the cheese business of ConAgra. We bought the only major cheese manufacturer in the South, from Winn Dixie. When we went to trade shows—especially when you're known as the sole supplier to McDonald's and Walmart—we were often the only major provider there because what we had in place was virtually

impossible to duplicate for national and regional grocery chains. Thus, we were very successful at attracting new prospects at these trade shows."

The Walmart Influence

The addition of Walmart as a major customer created a major challenge itself because they required three-day delivery terms, all over the country. Put this requirement in the context of Ottum's and Cawman's explanation of the challenges of inventorying so many individual SKUs!

Ottum said, "we had the shortest turn-around times in the industry, at two weeks. But two weeks is still two weeks, pretty long. Walmart got us to three days!" This drove a strategy of adding plants and distribution centers around the country. This wasn't as desirable for the smaller, multi-SKU Retail/Grocery Store chain business, but was ideal for the fast-food/Quick Service companies because their needs could be pre-manufactured and warehoused in coolers.

Failures

Not all ventures are successful, to be sure. In 1985, the company purchased California-based Westland Foods, a manufacturer of pre-cooked bacon, and named it the Pre-Cooked Foods division, intending to sell Bacon Bits and Bacon Slices to restaurants. It didn't take and the division was sold.

"Once we tried a new cheese product that our marketers said, 'should be gangbusters.' It involved a snack with brightly colored packaging. It bombed. That was part of my learning that 'should' is not a word you 'should' pay attention to," Meng said.

Another bomb: A peanut-butter-and-jelly sandwich offering.

Cost-Efficient Innovation Continues

As a private-label manufacturer, Schreiber's main differentiator would be innovations in cost and price.

• Bob Bush had invented the machine that could economically slice cheese and package it. At the store where the cheese is put on to the meat, … it's not quick to peel off each slice. Bob invented a machine that as it sliced each piece of cheese from the loaf, it would place it in the pile in a "staggered" fashion. Thus, it is much simpler and quicker for the worker to grab the piece of cheese and apply it.
     Result: Schreiber is the preferred supplier.

• For the grocery store/at-home market, homemakers want to buy the package, but only want one or two slices for a meal. Thus, Bob invented a machine that additionally would take each slice and wrap it in film before stacking it for the package. Thus, individually wrapped slices.
     Result: Schreiber is the preferred supplier.

• Some grocery chains, during the period when generics were taking hold, wanted to offer a lower-cost, lower-priced product that wasn't their store brand. So, Schreiber innovated by substituting vegetable fat for the more expensive butterfat. Lower cost, without a very discernable difference in taste.
     Result: Schreiber is the preferred supplier.

• Another lower-cost efficiency: Food regulations require a moisture content in various cheeses not to exceed various percentages. Say, 40%. Water is less expensive than anything, so you want to be as close to 40% as possible. If you're at 36%, you're not minimizing your costs. Thus, you want to discipline a process that gets you as close to 40% as possible. You never get to exactly 40%, but if you can average, say, 38% and never exceed 40%, you're approaching the lowest possible cost.

Tom Badciong

     Result: Schreiber remains the low-cost supplier.

The Tempe Plant: Installing GainSharing, and...
Not all the innovations were internally generated. In the early '80s, they learned of a new milk process that could segment the milk into its components much more cheaply called "ultra-filtration," developed in Australia, and largely unnoticed in the U.S. Tom Badciong was charged with developing a plant to test the process, which worked. Then, he was charged with developing a full-fledged cheddar-cheese processing plant using the technology located in Tempe, Arizona. It would give greater proximity to western markets and could tap into a huge dairy cow availability through a major coop there.

He also tried some innovations in how the plant was scheduled and managed. He set up four seven-person shifts working 12-hour days, charged with managing themselves. Each shift was allowed to do its own hiring, do its own disciplining, and make its own recommendations for compensation increases. If a member didn't show that day, they couldn't replace him. They would have to go with six, so cross-training was a premium.

In addition, he instituted a GainSharing incentive program there that had been tested successfully in the Monett, Missouri plant, with metric feedback by production line every day. "Our philosophy was that if people have skin in the game, they will always respond better." The program had five components: Two customer-driven ones, Fill Rates and Complaints, a moral one, Safety, and two shareholder ones, Productivity, and Raw Material Waste. Payouts were on a plant-wide basis, so every employee would get the same percentage increase.

By the late '90s, every Partner in the U.S. was covered by some sort of incentive plan.

The Green Bay Union Challenge
Over the years, the three-story Green Bay plant, the only unionized plant in the company, became the least and management began making alternative plans for it, which involved the Teamster Union agreement.

In 1986, the contract was renegotiated in a "horrendously conflictive process," recalled Jeff Ottum, who in 1990 would become the plant manager. Attorneys for Schreiber did the negotiating, eventually implementing a 10% reduction in pay, with no increases in any year for the six-year term of the contract. While those were implemented, there was no agreement on embracing the newly tested Gainsharing incentive program, nor several other procedural innovations. Obviously, it left an acrimonious feel within the workforce.

In 1990, Ottum took over with the objective of increasing the plant's customer focus, primarily by increasing the number of customer visits, and customer conversations with plant "Partners."

In 1992, when the contract was negotiated again, Ottum said, "attorneys were secondary. The negotiators were myself and Larry Ferguson, head of operations."

Recalls Ferguson: "We needed a different approach, as Jeff indicates. I was familiar with William Ury, co-author of the famous book on negotiations, Getting To Yes. I flew to Boston to meet with him, and then hired him to give us guidance."

They were able to bargain into the contract, for new employees, Schreiber's own 401(k) retirement plan, replacing the Teamster's notorious Central States Pension Fund for that group only. Schreiber assured the Teamster negotiators that if any Gainsharing program were instituted outside of the contract, that it would be additive to contract-negotiated pay levels. Also, it was for a three-year term, not a six-year one.

But challenges weren't over, as the plant was still the company's least efficient, making its ability to produce at a

Mark Peterson

competitive cost questionable. When the next contract was negotiated in 1995, with Mark Peterson as plant manager, the company proposed to close it and build a new one elsewhere in Green Bay that would be the most technologically advanced in the system. Employees would be assigned to jobs based on qualifications, not seniority.

Of course, the Union would have none of that. They recommended a No vote, which occurred. Later they wouldn't allow a re-vote. (This was the same local Teamsters leadership that Schneider was also dealing with concurrently.)

The company solution was to reduce the number of processes and amount of production in the plant to allow room for some additional higher-tech equipment, which reduced the employee count to 234 from 550.

Other Peterson initiatives as plant manager: To reduce the high recordable accident rate, 53 the year before he arrived, by emphasizing "Go home as safe as when you arrived." Within two years, the rate was less than 5 recordable's. Also, "I wanted to change the vernacular, from referring to 'bosses' to referring to 'leaders.' No one wants to have a boss. It took me three years to do that."

Larry Ferguson

Ferguson's Emphasis on Relationships

As Larry Ferguson assumed responsibility for all manufacturing in 1992, he had two major emphases. First, to sophisticate even further the emphasis on documenting and executing consistently across all plants the currently best processes. And second, to emphasize the primacy of performance by getting "the right people in the right job at the right time." This was critical because as a private label manufacturer, they had to be increasingly less costly than their customers, with consistently perfect quality measures.

He asserted when you emphasize performance using transparent metrics, you enhance morale because there can't be impressions of favoritism in rewards and promotions. He had a motto: "Personal Preference doesn't trump Professional Performance." "It sends the message that performance counts."

Ferguson's other major emphasis, born of his early learnings: Building Relationships.

"When I was in college, I became responsible for myself. When I took a job, I became responsible for others. To be effective at that, you have to be great at relationships."

"When I was in college, I became responsible for myself. When I took a job, I became responsible for others. To be effective at that, you have to be great at relationships. I was helped at that because my father moved us four times, and each time I had to create new

Nancy Armbrust

relationships with friends, and the same with promotions and moves at Schreiber. During that time, I learned, as Dale Carnegie said, the sweetest sound you hear is that of your own name. At Monett, I took photos of all the employees and studied them to learn their names, and then I learned the names of their family members. I really wanted to know them. That really helped. When you call a person by name and ask about their family by name, they know you care and feel the relationship with them is important. You can't get people to care about what you want them to until they know you care about them, and no one will care more than you do. Anyone can do this if you work at it. You have to learn how to express your authentic caring."

Sixteen weeks of a Dale Carnegie course helped him, he said.

Cementing The Culture

The influence of Jack Meng, other executives attest, is seen in many of the cultural elements that were initiated and/or made more institutionalized. Nancy Armbrust, the VP/Education & Community Relations, said: "We always had a focus on living to Core Values, centering on Partners, Family, Community, and God. They've always been paramount concerns of our leaders, but Jack was the one who 'put them on a Table,' really codified them."

Two of his mantras:

• "Respect The Past, But Don't Protect It."

• "Make Today Better Than Yesterday, and Tomorrow Better Than Today."

In addition, one of his best questions to analyze what was going on: "What Drives Work?"

Will this work be adding value that the customer is willing to pay for?

He was also instrumental in the early '80s in changing calling people Partners rather than Employees.

"Before, there were supervisors and managers, and nobody likes to be supervised or managed. If we're all working towards the same goals, the language needs to be in alignment, too." And, said Armbrust, in 1993, "Bob and Jack decided the operating units should be very involved in the fabric of their communities. That's when they created the position of VP/Education and Community as the face of that thrust. That became the major focus of the work I was charged with."

From Tom Badciong: "You could get fired for lying about why you were five minutes late, but you wouldn't be for making a million-dollar mistake if you treated it with transparency and as a learning process. Integrity is key. We are putting ingredients into food all over the world."

More on Jack Meng

Says Armbrust, "He was superb in creating a visual picture in our minds of what he was explaining to us ... whether it was around themes like personal responsibility or accountability, or even technical. He could simplify complex topics with great clarity. For example, in explaining the ESOP, he would emphasize the value of being an 'Owner/Operator' and the opportunity for 'creating individual wealth.'

"He professionalized our business systems, was a financial wizard, and really institutionalized our external, Customer-Focus."

Among his changes:

• Held salespeople to their contribution based on Variable Income. Variable revenue less variable costs. "They had no influence over Fixed Costs, which were usually allocated based on un-supportable logics and distorted analyses, so we controlled those at the corporate level."

"For Jack, it all starts with information. 'Information drives Beliefs, which drive Attitudes, which drive Behaviors ... which drive Results.'"

• Built an information system that reported performance on a Variable Contribution level. "We could rank each salesperson based on clean performance metrics. Bob asked, 'What are you going to do with this information?' 'I'm going to post the rankings?' 'Won't that make people feel bad?' 'Only the bottom five, and they may be in the wrong business anyway.'"

• He also emphasized keeping Partners informed. Initially, he did an annual Town Hall meeting at each facility. As that became unwieldy and too infrequent, he began doing monthly videos discussing what was going on in the company, plus any updates regarding operations, health insurance, and the like. (Today, the company relies on daily notices via the internal internet.)

• Per Tom Badciong: "For Jack, it all starts with information. 'Information drives Beliefs, which drive Attitudes, which drive Behaviors … which drive Results.'"

On Schreiber's Family-Friendly Culture, from Meng: "Despite our commitment to high ethics and values, at one point there were rumblings we weren't living up to them, and it seemed to be coming from single mothers in the workforce who as we know have unique pressures on them. Bob and I had a meeting with them and learned that there were mixed messages. Often leaders were imposing requirements they couldn't meet and would fear for their jobs. From that came a higher emphasis company-wide on being understanding about personal needs. We called it a 'Family-Friendly Culture.' The rule was to treat people from the perspective of the Partner, not the company.

"But here's the benefit. We had an accountant who was a single mother, who had to leave early to catch the bus to pick up her child. We allowed that. And when month-end occurred, she would come in at 3 AM several days, and get our month-end reports out a day earlier than they ever had before."

Ron Dunford

CEO Transitions ... and Growth

In 1985 Bob Bush went to Meng and said he wanted him to be his successor. Meng ran the company until 1999 when the ESOP was completed. He was followed by Larry Ferguson, the operations and strategy guru, who served until 2007, a short spell by David Pozniak, who is given credit for beginning the international push, until he got sick, and then Mike Haddad, the first to come from the sales side of the business, who made them "Modern and Global," from 2009 until 2019. Today, Ron Dunford, with sales as well as an international operations background, is the CEO.

Schreiber crossed the $1 billion sales level in 1993, $2 billion in 2000, $4 billion in 2008, and over $6 billion today. In 2009 when Haddad became CEO, the international business produced 11% of earnings, and when he retired in 2019, it was 40%. Of the 8,800 Partners, 3,500 worked outside the U.S.

Today, Schreiber operates 16 plants in the U.S., plus nine Distribution Centers, making it one day away from any location in the U.S. With additional plants in 11 other countries.

The ESOP

Over the years, since 1962 when the 13 original executives bought stock, key executives were offered shares in the company at the prevailing book value, usually using loans provided by Kellogg Bank and its successor, Associated Bank. Says Meng:

"Keep in mind that we were doing really well, compounding our bottom line at a 16% annual rate, meaning our value kept doubling in less than every five years. The shares were becoming expensive not only for an executive to buy in but for the company to payout a stock-owning executive at retirement. We were also aware of a legal requirement that says if you have more than a certain number of shareholders (we had about 270 at the time), you have to disclose your financial performance publicly. We didn't want to get to that point."

The solution, after considerable analysis: The company was "sold" to a 100% Employee Stock Ownership Plan (ESOP) in 1999. That means every employee, once vested, shares in the increased market value of the company and gets paid out upon retirement.

This also importantly assures the company will probably never be sold but will remain headquartered in Green Bay, similar to the current KI status. The plan is only applicable to U.S. employees because its tax advantages exist under U.S. law; employees in other countries are covered under other profit-sharing plans.

Says former CEO Mike Haddad, "The ESOP commits to redeem the retiring shareholder's shares. That creates debt which the ESOP must pay down from future profits, but it gives liquidity to the retirement sale event."

(See appendices for more information about how the ESOP works, including its drawbacks.)

> *"I told the Board, 'Get ready to spend $200 million in buying into these businesses.' We started with Cream Cheese.*

Adding New Products: Cream Cheese

Ferguson, who became CEO in 1999, succeeding Meng, said: "We had 90% of the processed cheese market, and for growth, I wanted to take us from being a Cheese company to being a Dairy company. Our strengths were in Distribution (We were in almost every retail outlet in the U.S), and in R&D (We were experts in dairy protein and dairy fat). Dairy protein and fat, which are needed for Cheese, are the same elements that constitute Cream Cheese and Yogurt. It all fit. What part of milk isn't needed for one, can be used for the other.

"I told the Board, 'Get ready to spend $200 million in buying into these businesses.' We started with Cream Cheese. I approached a French company and, U.S.-based Raskas for joint ventures, but they didn't bite. (Raskas was a family-owned $180 million operation and made almost 80% of the private label cream cheese in America.) So, we bought Lov-It Creamery in Green Bay, which made both butter and cream cheese, to let everyone know we meant it; that put us in the cream cheese business. Then, we purchased the cream cheese part of Beatrice.

The main component was family-owned Raskas Foods of St. Louis, which eventually became amenable to being purchased. The last piece, in 2004, was Level Valley here in Wisconsin, the second-largest producer after Raskas. That gave us 95% of all the U.S. cream cheese business that wasn't Kraft's Philadelphia."

"But buying a business is easy. The next problem is assimilating it into your organization so that it is additive. And after that, the challenge is optimizing to make the parts work together as well as they can. These efforts take years. It took us 4-5 years before we properly assimilated and optimized our Cream Cheese initiative.

"One big help was that we put every piece on the same information system—Oracle. Integrating Oracle as our ERP took us ten years. But there was no exception. Every acquisition went on the same information system. That was critical."

And Yogurt!

According to Ron Dunford, Ferguson's promotion of the Yogurt strategy wasn't an easy one. The company had its expertise, and why risk such a major bet. But Ferguson was adamant. In one meeting, he said, "We're going to do it. Someday, we'll be a Yogurt company that also sells Cheese."

(Of interest, today, in 2021, Yogurt revenues about equal cheese revenues.)

Dunford continued, "Larry targeted Hilltop Valley Yogurt, a small manufacturer in Richland Center, Wisconsin. Dan LaValley, the CEO, was planning on building a second plant in Arizona. Larry approached him about delaying that decision and said 'Come with us to our Logan, Utah, plant, and see how we operate. Maybe you'll consider becoming part of us.' So, we flew with Dan out to Logan, and by the time we landed he was pretty much committed, and after the tour, he did commit. We made him head of our yogurt business and built that second plant adjoining our Logan facility. We were in the yogurt business."

The yogurt entry began in 2005. Another key, though, was a very large acquisition of a competitor in 2011, making Schreiber tied for being the second-largest yogurt producer in the U.S. Dannon was the largest. In 2014, it entered the European market in a big way, purchasing plants in Slovakia and Spain, cementing its place as one of the largest yogurt producers in the world, except you don't see it because it's not a Schreiber brand. Sometimes, when you see the Dannon brand, the yogurt inside the package is made by Schreiber.

Expanding Internationally

The international business began with starts and pullbacks. A Mexico City plant had been opened in 1980, then closed in 1982. A Northern Ireland plant lasted from 1980 to 1985.

But then, expansion took off in earnest as Schreiber followed its major customers to other countries. As McDonald's grew overseas, so did Schreiber, beginning with a German joint venture and a Saudi Arabia operation in 1992, followed by a joint venture in India in 1996, and into Brazil in 1999.

The period under Larry Ferguson was a very major growth spurt. There are major challenges in managing effectively fast growth. But because you're following the customers, businesses have to make it happen effectively to maintain the business. A perfect storm of opportunities allowed this growth.

First, it was an extraordinary expansion period for the major "Quick Service" chains (McDonald's, Subway, Burger King, Wendy's, and many others). At the same time, Walmart began increasing its commitment to the food business.

So, by 2006, the company had plants in Mexico, Brazil, Germany, and India.

It was also a time of customer dominance. "As these now-becoming- worldwide customers were expanding ... think Walmart, Costco, Subway, McDonald's ... they were at the same time necessarily fanatical about supply chain efficiency. They pretty much know what the costs were and what the pricing needed to be for us to succeed, so they worked closely with us to create cost savings wherever possible. We were becoming a Logistics company driven by Technology," said Haddad.

When Haddad became CEO in 2009, he targeted continuing global expansion as one of his two major objectives.

Dunford recalled, "His approach was to increase Schreiber's visibility as a player, and to meet as many of the other players in the dairy business as possible, let them know what we are trying to do expansion-wise, and if they got to the point of wanting to sell, to be sure to talk to us. We began acquiring Dannon plants in Europe, several of the best cheese processing plants in France, and elsewhere. We added a plant in Latin America and two more in India."

Haddad said, "The first major one was Dannon Yogurt, which had a plant in Germany, and we already had the U.S. relationship. We asked them what shortfalls they were seeing with their current vendors that Schreiber was strong in, usually in the Values we brought to our relationships and marketplaces, which they didn't find as strong in their current suppliers. That was our inroad. It motivated us to open seven more plants producing Dannon's formula. We also then could use these plants to efficiently produce cheese for others."

Today, the company has additional plants in India, as well as in Austria, Bulgaria, the Czech Republic, Portugal, Spain, Mexico, and Uruguay.

The new Schreiber headquarters building in downtown Green Bay.

New Headquarters Building

Mike Haddad's mantra was "Modern ... and Global." He invested huge dollars in making the company more sophisticated, incorporating robotics and other automation to make the company more efficient and profitable.

The new Headquarters building in Green Bay is one of his biggest feats. Besides consolidating operations from several disparate locations into one facility, it has several unique features. The IT/Communications area directly connects the company with every plant, distribution center, and office in the world. There is a duplicate, redundant capability in Milwaukee.

In addition, there is a full-blown, modern, high-tech dairy in the building where they can do any research they want, as well as a full-blown lab with Ph.D.'s where they can do cutting-edge research.

All the major "Quick Serve" chains have their own kitchen area with all of their own cooking equipment. Schreiber can replicate everything they do in their stores.

Going Modern also meant ramping up two other initiatives. They were both part of the Schreiber Value concerns, but their societal emphasis required institutionalizing them even more:

Diversity and Inclusion, and Environmental/Social/Governance (ESG).

"We became more attuned to environmental impacts. The things you can't see. We created a Director, Environmental Programs, which now does full ESG audits. If you aren't, the big companies won't even begin talking with you," said Haddad.

More About Bob Bush

• "He was the quintessential Question-Asker!! Because he was a very linear thinker, very logical, he usually had a very good sense of the sequence of events that had to happen, and therefore knew the questions to ask to determine if the situations had been sufficiently thought out. Or he was just curious about what the person was doing. Or, when he learned something new, he would ask if you were aware of it. If not, he would explain it to you."

• "He cared about adding real talent. He looked for people who could juggle five or six balls in the air at one time. At that time, there was no formal training program. Throw us in the lake and let us swim."

• "He was an advocate of obtaining patents to protect a competitive differentiation, and then suing to enforce them."

• "Because of his personal emphasis on looking for technical improvements, he stimulated people to be innovative."

• "He would know what he didn't know or wasn't good at and would find and hire people who were the best at it. That's how he developed a leadership team that could drive Schreiber's growth. He also would hire smart people when they were available, often before they were needed ... so they could adapt to the culture and be ready when they were needed."

• "He genuinely knew that every job was important. People who design processes know that." Says Tracy, "On Saturdays, sometimes I would accompany him to the plant. He would go to each department in turn and ask how it was going and he could call people by their names (until the company got too big)."

• "He was an early proponent of the Kepner-Tregoe decision-making process. He even taught it to his children, and they still use that thinking process today when making decisions."

• "He didn't promote technology for its own sake, but rather technology that would make a difference in what we did."

• "If you worked around Bob, you adhered to the organization's principles, including how to treat people. As board chair of Bellin Hospital, he was told once of a surgeon who wasn't following all of the protocols, and that nurses had tactfully advised him of the variances. "Tell him today is the last day he works at Bellin Hospital!'"

• "Yes, he could be intimidating. He would drop his glasses down on his nose and look directly at you. There wouldn't be any B.S. But he was flexible. One time, I took initiative, believing in a new approach, and ordered some equipment without his knowledge and then argued to him about how my idea would be the best approach. Finally, he told me to go ahead and asked how quickly we could get equipment in. I took him to the window and showed him the equipment that had just arrived. He started laughing."

• "He was always looking for ways to hurt the competition, always seeking that leading edge."

• "You take care of this company, and this company will take care of you."

• "He was Mr. Integrity. He would always put the company and the people over himself and his own honor."

• "He was proud that the company was built on a foundation of handshakes with suppliers and to customers, not contracts."

• "When visiting a plant, it wasn't just to see how the equipment he designed was running but talk to the people who were running it and everyone else."

• "As we added plants in other communities, he wanted to make sure that, as part of our community relations, we were doing something for the less well-off in those communities."

• "If Bob had a suggestion during a plant tour, you listened because it would invariably be a good suggestion. He wasn't trying to find fault, but he could see things that the rest of us didn't."

Takeaways

If you got this far in this book of stories, you are a natural learner. You are reading these stories while looking for lessons. Lessons that support what you're already doing. And lessons that say, "Hey, I need to do that ... or more of that!" Too, you may be thinking that some of the people in your own organization need to be exposed to these stories, of these successful journeys to success.

Here are some lessons embedded in these stories. What others do you see?

Powerfully Driven

First, these CEOs were powerfully driven. They were unrelenting. They pushed people and often asked more than was reasonable, especially of their best people, the ones they could rely on the most. Sometimes they were even abusive in what they asked, sometimes unfortunately purposefully so.

Compelling Missions And Visions

Secondly, this worked because their Missions and the associated Visions were ones that enchanted all their direct reports; they were compelling. They were pushing to be successful on a very large stage, from little Green Bay. They were always striving to be more effective at serving their customers ... or implementing the best of the new operational ideas. They were creating customers of the biggest names in their marketplaces; they weren't bashful about approaching the biggest and best. Critically, everyone was thoughtful and smart about how they did

147

it. They were realistic and practical. They were humble, resolute, and represented the best of Wisconsin's touted work ethic. It came naturally.

Schreiber was providing cheese to McDonald's in the 1960s.

Schneider Logistics went after 3M and GM.

KI was the furniture supplier of choice to Sun Microsystems and Microsoft in their heyday.

Constantly Seeking Breakthroughs

Thirdly, they were changing their industries. They were coming up with new ideas and implementing them.

AMS was the first to introduce both the Health Insurance Card and Co-Pays, which we all use today.

Schneider was the first to introduce microwave communications/tracking systems so you knew where every truck was and could communicate directly to the drivers.

Fort Howard introduced paper recycling when it wasn't a "thing" and dominated as the low-cost provider—and still does.

Schreiber used a core values-based culture to attract innovative thinkers.

KI was the first to use high chair fashion designers to differentiate it from the billion-dollar players.

Spreading The Wealth

Fourth, internally they spread the wealth through Gain-Sharing/Profit-Sharing and other incentive plans, so a wide group of leaders, and often all employees, could benefit from the financial performance of the organization. Fort Howard for a long time had its Goodwill Bonus. Schreiber by 1999 had every employee on an incentive reward plan, and both Schreiber and KI now have 100% ESOPs where all employees can benefit from the increase of the organization's market value.

Continuous Improvement

Fifth, at some point, they switched from an Inward focus to an Outward one. Their initial differentiator, which got them business for decades, were usually a capability of excellent operational performance.

Fort Howard was the low-cost provider in the industry with relatively undifferentiated products for industrial/commercial uses.

Schreiber made other companies' products, and a required differentiator besides appropriate quality was being low cost compared to competitors.

Schneider worked feverishly to drive cost out of its trucking so it could compete with non-union competitors.

AMS made sure its services to its agents, its "ease of doing business," would attract them because its product costs didn't.

KI used transparency of cost information to the lowest level as a driver for acute attention to efficiencies.

Several very early adopted the Lean concepts which used high quality to drive low cost.

Customer Focus

And each, at some point, re-focused to start with customer needs/wants as their first concern. "We start with the customer, and then work back," said Jack Meng.

KI in the early 1990s when it transformed itself into a Customer Of One focus, which differentiated it completely from competitors.

Schreiber in the 1980s struggled financially when Kraft targeted their business, and quickly switched to a market-focused regime.

Schneider had always had a strategy of adding busy routes through acquisition, but as they converted to non-union, they were very strategic in where they set up major terminals, at important interstate intersections to serve routes of major customers.

AMS didn't really have a point of conversion. Ron and Wally, in the insurance business, were always focused on the needs of their small business policyholders and looking to solve problems for them.

Whereas Fort Howard had never completely converted to a consumer dominance, but in the 1980s it nevertheless began successfully and with good margins growing consumer-focused products.

Strategy, Values Set Early

For some, the principal strategy and values were set early, often by their predecessors. They took over, maintained the core, and built on it.

Austin Cofrin set the Fort Howard strategy of being low cost by recycling paper and being secretive.

Mer Bush set the "Sixteen Ounces To The Pound" ethic that created the foundation of integrity.

Al Krueger was already providing tables and chairs on a national basis when Dick Resch arrived.

The mantra in Colleen and Ron Weyers living room headquarters was Have Fun!

Don Schneider set the strategy of Become Non-Union using the values of being Transparent and Forthright.

Their Journeys Were Different.

They didn't all come at their businesses with familiarity.

• Bob Bush was the son of Mer Bush and grew up within the cheese business.

• Paul Schierl's father was in paper manufacturing in Appleton.

• Don Schneider's father built a struggling trucking firm from scratch.

But ...

• Ron Weyers and Wally Hilliard came from farm backgrounds ... but were quick studies of what didn't work.

• Dick Resch's parents were teachers and communicators, but he was ambitious and a quick learner.

GREAT BUSINESS PEOPLE

They were all GREAT BUSINESS PEOPLE! They relished and thrived on the Great Game of Business. They understood all its various elements. They used that understanding as a foundation, as the parameters, for their drive to dominate, to WIN AT THE GAME! Even when they didn't win, they analyzed why and tried another path. They were unstoppable!

A Bit About What Else

Most of these lessons have been around for a while. We just need to apply them and do it unrelentingly. But a few things may not have been critical in some of the marketplaces of yesterday, but truly are critical today. Here are three:

Succession Planning and Organizational Development

People would much rather work for a company that has a plan for developing them. "We can't promise you employment, but we can promise you employability." Schneider was perhaps the most complete in developing training/development programs during those times. Others depended on more informal development, more on-the-job. But the fact is that with mobility today, companies need to have at least several people in the training/development journey for each critical position. That means structured Succession Planning, targeting specific individuals as backups to be trained/developed. And that development program should be looking at a host of critical leadership skills that can only be refined through practice. There are specific, structured ways to be doing this. Too many leaders today say they are doing this informally. That's not enough. They need to be perceived by their employees as doing it in a structured way and perceived in the marketplace of prospective employees as having these in place.

Using Technology To Disrupt

Today, just staying even with the ways of customers and competitors requires substantial investment in threshold technology. To assure that you will survive requires being proactive about disrupting, figuring out things you can do that customers don't even know they need, or are available to them. Typically, this means more sophisticated analysis and use of data, providing information to customers and suppliers that make them more successful. All this means you need to do what Ron and Wally did intuitively back in the 1970s: Watch your customers and suppliers closely for what they are doing, and how they might be able to do it better or serve their customers better than a competitor might. Today, besides Augmented Reality, 3D Printing, and others, your disruptor might be sitting in your data base about your customer. Be proactive about this. Do brainstorming with your customer-facing people. Ask the doers at customers, suppliers and inside your own organization what might help them be more efficient or effective. Have "Tell Me More ..." conversations with the technology gurus in your area.

What's Coming At You

We can get too comfortable, and miss the signals that others aren't missing about a potential disruptor, perhaps initiated in another industry or another country. Instead of being a disruptor, we become the disrupted. Consider embracing techniques like Foresight Analysis, currently being taught by Envision Greater Green Bay, that take your scanning of the environment from haphazard and "when time allows" to a more structured approach, involving more of your senior leaders, that forces paying attention to signals, and hopefully forces testing new approaches and the resulting disruptive strategic initiatives.

There are state-of-the-art resources here in Northeast Wisconsin for each of these initiatives. Embrace them, just as our predecessors did proactively thirty years ago.

What Are Your Takeaways?
When Are YOU Going To Start?

Special Thanks for the content of this Appendix to Brian Liddy and Nick Guerrieri, CFOs at Schreiber and KI, respectively, when their respective ESOPs were put in place.

Thank you to Mark Olsen, Former CFO of KI who was very involved with the 1980s' LBOs, for his insight and experience in developing this item.

The Fort Howard data is from publicly available documents.

Appendices

Appendix I: Anatomy of an LBO

Within this book, both Fort Howard and KI consummated Leveraged Buyouts during the 1980s, a time when they were a relatively rare form of business financing.

They are typically done so that the existing management of the company can purchase the company from its actual owners, some of whom may be the same people as management, and some may also be passive shareholders. Because lenders usually lend a majority of the transaction value—in the 80% to 90% range of the buyout—they require that the management be competent, with a strong belief in their ability to grow the company significantly in order to generate enough profits or cash flow to pay off the debt, which often carries a high-interest rate, as well as warrants for future stock purchases.

Generally, the group leading the LBO will create a unique company whose sole purpose is to consummate the transaction. It will then be merged into the operating company with the operating company as the surviving organization. In Fort Howard's case, the unique company was called FH Acquisition Corp. (In the case of KI, it was KI Holdings, Inc.) There was a group of investment companies putting the deal together, and they provided the equity part of the transaction as part of FH Acquisition Co.'s capitalization. In Fort Howard's case, this amount was $450 million.

The people providing the $450 million are the new owners of the company. They will probably issue shares to the owners (themselves) in the proportion that each provide their part of the $450 million.

Thus, in Fort Howard's case, Morgan Stanley Leveraged Equity Fund II, Limited Partnership, plus capital from the Morgan Stanley parent, would become the principal owner with 73.5% of the shares. That group would effectively control the fortunes of the company, with its leader being the de facto Board Chairman. (They would ratify the management team in its official roles, including one of them, Paul Schierl, as CEO.)

Then, they seek lenders to provide the rest of the probable transaction cost as debt. That debt comes in multiple forms, depending on whether it has collateral backing it (or not in case of bankruptcy or default).

In Fort Howard's case, the debt forms were forecast to look like this:

Bank Financing	$2,025,000,000
Subordinated Debt	1,492,000,000
Existing Debt	235,000,000
Total Debt	$3,752,000,000
Stockholders' Equity	450,000,000
Total Capitalization	$4,202,000,000

Now, what is the value of the transaction?

It is the total dollars required to reimburse (buyout) the current stockholders/owners—plus an additional amount provided for additional future uses, providing security. In Fort Howard's case, the price per share was set at $53, and about 67,000,000 shares were outstanding, making the Buyout value $3.6 billion.

The financing package, therefore, would be sufficient to finance the buyout and still provide a strong but leveraged Balance Sheet.

There is another requirement by the major investors: That the senior management is also an investor in the project, both supplying the funds, so they have a stake in its future, and have some ownership, so that they have incentive to make the project work.

In Fort Howard's case, three senior executives participated, and purchased 3.8% of the outstanding shares for $17.1 million—most of their purchase price they financed by loans. In addition, there was an agreement to set aside up to 2.6% of the shares for purchase by other senior management members after the sale and merger were consummated; and, an agreement to provide even more shares for management performance incentives later on.

In the case of KI, the senior leadership purchased the company in 1981 from the Krueger family with Northwest Mutual Life holding a large portion of the debt with warrants attached to the debt. In addition, three regional banks, led by M&I Marshall and Ilsley Bank out of Milwaukee, provided the balance of the debt. Seven members of management led by Dick Resch pooled their resources and provided the needed equity to complete the funding of the purchase of the company. This eventually led to a second leveraged buyout in 1986 in which management 'bought out' the NML portion of the debt. This left the company in the hands of management, albeit with a large debt on the balance sheet, but in complete control of the ownership of KI going forward.

Appendix II: Anatomy of an ESOP

Both Schreiber, in 1999, and KI, in 2018, re-composed their ownership as 100% Employee Stock Ownership Plan (ESOP). Legally, it's a retirement plan. 100% means that all employees, once fully vested, are included, and their accounts will be fully paid to them upon retirement.

In both cases, the main reason driving the change was to provide a mechanism to buy out the shares of retiring shareholders. But just as important, and critical going forward, was to provide an ownership mentality culture for All employees. The latter was made immeasurably easier because these companies, for more than the previous decade, had managed profit-sharing plans as well as customer-focused cultures that engaged employees at a high level. To varying degrees, they already had elements of an ownership mentality.

A third reason for each company was a desire to keep the headquarters in Green Bay.

When you have a 100% ESOP, meaning that all employees are "owners," does not mean they have the attributes of normal owners. Rather, it means they are beneficiaries of the Trust that owns the company. They are still employees, who are subject to performance requirements.

They are beneficiaries because they own a percentage of the company whose amount will likely increase as the company's fortunes increase, which will be paid out to them when they leave. The value of their percentage will not be based on the increases in the actual dollar profitability of the company (Book Value). Rather, the amount will be based on the Market Value of the company at the beginning of the year when the payout occurs. This usually happens upon retirement, but could be whenever they quit.

Each year-end, the company is "valued" by an independent valuation consultant engaged by the Trustee.

The Trustee is the person who has the fiduciary responsibility to ensure the company is run for the benefit of the Trust participants, which are all eligible employees. But he does not "run" the company. Instead, he approves the members of the Board of Directors, and they select the CEO, who is the person who "runs" the company.

In both Schreiber's and KI's plans, the Trustee is an executive of a company called GreatBanc Trust Co., which has a very deserved reputation of effective fiduciary guidance acting as Trustees. They also keep the retirement plan in compliance with the Department of Labor and IRS regulations, such as ERISA. Each company has a retirement plan committee that recommends whether the Trustee should be retained each year.

The names of the owning trusts of the two companies are the KI ESOP Trust and the Schreiber Foods, Inc. Employee Stock Ownership Plan.

Each year, the Trust is funded from company profits, but usually only to the amount needed to payout to retiring and quitting shareholders. The rest of the profit dollars remain with the company.

Both KI and Schreiber have underlying GainSharing/Profit-Sharing Plans and other incentive plans for employees and some leaders. These continue to payout annually as normal. The ESOP payout is clearly a retirement program.

Why An ESOP?

The ESOP program as a "qualified retirement plan" designed to stimulate employee ownership was created by Congress in 1974. The incentive is that if a company is an ESOP company, their year-end profits are not taxed. Instead, the company value, based on the market value appraisal, is imbued in each employee's stock ownership account. When they take the payout, that payout will then be taxed at the individual's applicable tax rate. In effect, the company is not burdened with the tax cost; instead, it is deferred until the payout. The employee is informed annually of their account value when the valuation is completed.

The Transition to the ESOP

The first step of the Transition is to set up the Trust, to which the company will soon be "sold."

The second step is for the Trust to borrow money to pay off the current company owner- shareholders. Determining the share values is a complicated enterprise as it must pass the muster of the Trustee's decision that the Trust will take on only a reasonable amount of debt to provide that funding. The Board will have its lawyers, and the Trust or Trustee will have its lawyers. The company will retain a consulting company experienced in determining "fair value" after comparisons to comparable situations. (This is important because if it isn't "fair," it can't be logically defended in a disgruntled shareholder suit. It needs to be considered "fair" by all parties.) There's another attorney, too: One who makes sure that federal regulations under ERISA are being met. Then, an investment firm is hired to manage the financing. Typically, the shareholders will be paid a combination of actual cash as well as subordinated notes (debt). If some shareholders' amounts are very large, the payout may be over several years to reduce the new company's cash flow challenge.

(If the company has sizeable cash reserves, it may use some of this to pay off the shareholders, reducing the amount of needed debt.)

The dollars involved for both Schreiber and KI were very considerable. For example, Schreiber's ESOP is considered one of the Top Ten in the nation in size, and KI's is in the Top 45 or so.

The third step is for the company to be "sold" to the Trust, which will now be the owner of 100% of the company's shares. There will never be any more independent shareholders of the new company. Only vested employees.

Finally, formally, the Trustee will appoint the Board of Directors, who will appoint the CEO and other officers of the company.

Over time, the Trustee and the Board members will make annual decisions regarding funding from the ongoing enterprise to pay off the debt.

Employees' share values are reported to them at least annually. The values, as mentioned, are based on an independent analysis of the market value of the company—what it would yield if sold. These days, the market value is often much larger than the book value, making it a very lucrative investment for the employee. Indeed, for Schreiber, the Market Value is currently several times larger than the Book Value.

The Downside

Like every plan that distributes profits, it is a drain on the company's cash reserves which are then not available for other business development uses. In the case of the ESOP, the amount paid out can be a lot as the company's market value continues to rise. As older employees retire, this "hit" can be significant. (A good one for the retiring employee, of course!) Managing this for every ESOP is a major task as time goes on.

ESOPs can be very successful, but they can be a constraint in some ways including the ability to raise additional capital. They are not always a panacea.

Acknowledgements

There are, of course, many. There always are.

There are the people around me, who put up with me, including the time it took to develop the materials for this book. Those people are really a person: Kitty, my wife and soulmate who is immensely tolerant, and encouraged me all the way.

There are the members of my TEC/Vistage CEO Groups and the Senior Marketing/Sales Executive Group who became my friends as they allowed me to be part of their lives and live many of their travails with them.

There are the people listed in each chapter, who took their time to reminisce about this very impactful time in their life. I asked them to remember back 20-45 years, Wow! ... And they could! And even though many did not know me, they trusted that in the end I would represent them and their situation well. I did return my drafts to them so they could improve both the accuracy and context of what I wrote.

When you are going through something, you deal with the day-to-day and think a bit about tomorrow, but rarely with the full perspective you have when looking back a decade or so, and being able to compare those times with other times. They did a phenomenal job, just doing their job.

I spent thirty years facilitating CEO Groups for The Executive Committee (TEC) and Vistage, with more than a hundred CEOs as members over those years. That experience and those friendships were the key to my ability to understand what these people had to say, and to interpret it correctly.

There is my good friend, Ken Utech, with whom I co-authored a previous book, who has spent the last twenty years correcting my insights, to my benefit.

To Lynn and Kevin Hesness, principals of Seaway Printing, who have donated the printing of these books. As well as Denis Kreft, principal with Imaginasium, who donated development of the website to allow online ordering.

Also, to Dr. Rebeccca Meacham's Teaching Press at UW—Green Bay, a group of student-interns she hires to get actual practice editing and publishing the book. They have the software and the printing equipment to do this. This is entirely a product of their effort, from receipt of my text through delivery of the finished book. In addition, the Press interns have had a great time figuring out how to promote the book, to give it visibility.

And to Tim Weyenberg, who led me to them after they did the same with his book of poetry.

And there is YOU! Hopefully, you will be able to read these stories and read between the lines and take away some ideas that will be very useful for you going forward. There is a lot of teaching in these stories.

I trust this will be a useful resource.

Phil Hauck
Fall 2021